VIRTUAL WOMF

Changing Sex

VIRTUAL WOMEN: LADYBOYS

Changing Sex in Thailand

Dr Anne Beaumont, PhD

Annie Beaumont
x

YOUCAXTON PUBLICATIONS

OXFORD & SHREWSBURY

ISBN 978-1-909644-23-6
Printed and bound in Great Britain.

Dedication

Firstly, I dedicate this work to all the British transsexual women and Ladyboys who so willingly and freely shared their stories with me. Without you, this work would not be possible. Thank you and *Khorp khun mahk ka!*

Secondly, I dedicate this book to my wonderful family. My fondest love goes to:

My daughter, Dr Nicola-Anne Magnusson and her husband, Rune Magnusson, together with my truly amazing grandsons, Alexander Magnusson and Oliver Magnusson.

To my son, Dean Beaumont and his wife, Joanne, together with, Kirstie-Anne, Laura and James, I send my love, as always.

Acknowledgements

So many people have been a significant presence and influence during my research and the writing of this book. Without their advice, support and interest in my scholarly journey, this work would never have reached fruition. There are far too many to mention here, however, my grateful thanks go to:

Professor Ken Plummer (Essex University)
Dr Colin Samson (Essex University)
Professor Diane Elson (Essex University)
Professor Joan Busfield (Essex University)
Dr Heather Montgomery (The Open University)
Ms Rowena Macawley (Essex University)
Dr Berenice Rivera Macias
Dr Chrissie Rogers
Dr Beverley Chaplin
Professor Milton Diamond, University of Hawai'i
Professor Peter Jackson, Australian National University
Bernard and Terry Reed, GIRES
Ms Gill Dalton
Rebekah Alexander-Brown
Bob Fowke, YouCaxton Publications

Contents

Foreword

The title of the book, 'Virtual Women' derives from the fact that, as I see it, the person transitioning from one gender to another can only achieve an *approximation* of a change of sex. Another fact is that, as I will show, such categories of women have not been fully accepted, at a social level, as belonging to the female gender category. Transgendered embodiment has to be constantly negotiated and renegotiated. Employing a term from anthropologist Mary Douglas, I argue that transsexual women are, 'matter out of place'. They hold no legitimate gender but rather they dwell on the margins of gender. Hence, as transsexual women cannot be medically transformed completely to female and struggle for acceptance within the gender borders of womanhood, they are, then, to unashamedly borrow a term from cyber-speak, virtual women.

The purpose of this book is to tell the stories of the life experiences of those persons known medically as 'transsexual' or 'transgender'. In Thailand, such persons are known as *Kathoey* or 'Ladyboys'.

Personal Preface

This book has been a long time in gestation. It began long ago, when, as a little girl then living in a children's home, I was taken to the pantomime. I saw a pretty lady on the stage. She was singing and telling jokes, making the audience laugh. The lady asked for a child from the audience to sing with her. The brave child would win a prize. With great trepidation I ascended the steps and, once I was up there, I trembled at the sight of the darkened audience. The lady meanwhile, resplendent in long, voluminous dress, red cheeks and lipstick, big hair and eyelashes, picked me up so that I could reach the microphone. My face was now at the same level as hers and I was horror-struck to realise that this was not a lady but a grotesquely made-up man. Revulsion filled me, I felt betrayed and fooled and angry. How dare he/she? How dare a man deceive people into believing that he was a female? It is entirely possible that I was the only person in the whole theatre who did not know that the pantomime Dame is always a man!

Men and women have been cross-dressing in pantomime and drama for centuries. There's nothing new in it. Female actors play the handsome prince in stage productions such as Sleeping Beauty and Snow White and the Seven Dwarfs and a female plays the male hero (the cat named Dick) in the pantomime Dick Whittington. In Peter Pan the hero of that name is always played by a female. Conversely, males act as 'women' on stage – the pantomime Dame, the ugly sisters in Cinderella and Widow Twanky in Aladdin ... it goes on and on...

But whereas females playing male roles in pantomime are glamorous, males playing females project themselves as grotesque caricatures and play it for laughs. It seems to be culturally and socially acceptable for females to wear masculine clothing, but unacceptable for males to take on the role of the female sex. A man dressed as a woman (even a pantomime Dame) flies in the face of our accepted, taken-for-granted gender norms.

This book is about men who not only want to be women, but believe themselves to be truly women, women who, through some freakish accident of birth, have been born in the wrong body. It traces the difficulties they face on the road to transition as they migrate from male to female and it looks at the cultural transgender phenomenon in Thailand, where omnipresent beings blend genders: the Kathoey – known as Ladyboys – who live their lives betwixt and between in sex.

Dr Anne Beaumont, Ph.D.
Norfolk, March 2014

CHAPTER ONE
Introducing the Transgender Phenomenon

This book explores the transgender phenomenon in the very different cultural settings of England and Thailand. I situate myself here as dwelling between the interdisciplinary borders of social anthropology and medical sociology. 'Transgender' describes, broadly, a change of sex whether partially or more fully, part-time or full-time. Transgender can be viewed as a kind of 'umbrella' term, describing the transsexual, the transvestite, the drag queen or the drag king. The term 'transsexual', however, describes, for me, the person who feels that they were born with the wrong gendered body; a body that does not match their gender identity. One's 'gender identity' can be described as one's inner knowing of the gender to which they belong — that is, whether they are male or female. A transsexual person feels intense discomfort with their morphological body and seeks to change it permanently, through genital and other surgeries, in order to bring it in line with their gender identity. Drawing on the narratives of the participants of my study, I investigate the social worlds of those individuals who seek to change their bodily sex from male to female (often referred to as 'transsexual women' or 'transwomen') in England and 'Ladyboys' (known locally as 'kathoey') in Thailand and the transitional journeys that take them from 'male' to 'female'.

It is very difficult to satisfactorily answer the question, *'What is a woman?'* 'Woman' does not necessarily reflect an essentialist or biological status, but rather a social category, whereas 'female' for me represents a biological category. Such an explanation seems straightforward enough. However, the picture is more complex than this very simplistic explanation would suggest. 'Gender' represents the social classification of 'woman' or 'man', whereas 'sex' refers to the biological category, female or male (which is, of course, also a socially constructed category). Being a 'woman' however, does not automatically assume a 'female' sexed embodiment. Every person experiences the body physically and biologically. However, we also experience our bodies socially and psychologically, and these four aspects together — the physical, the biological, the social and the psychological — are what we experience as 'embodiment'. If sex and gender are understood in terms of a 'bipolar' paradigm, then those who cross the gender borders cause chaos to the bipolarized social construction of sex and gender. In Western society, such a person is known as a 'male-to-female transsexual', a 'transsexual woman', or a 'transwoman'. A transwoman has no female reproductive organs, although she may well have hormone or surgically induced breasts and constructed 'female-type' genitalia. The fact that her original bodily phenotype was male should not repudiate her social status as a 'woman', albeit she is a 'trans'-woman. She remains an approximation of a woman: what I would call a *Virtual Woman*. However, there are many 'biological' women whose bodies are devoid of reproductive organs, either as a result of disease, sex reassignment surgery (as in the case of a female-to-male transsexual man) or congenital 'abnormality'. Does a hysterectomized woman, for example, lose her right to her social status as a woman just because she no longer has a womb? The same could be said for women who have undergone surgery to remove breasts because of cancer. Does the mere absence of womb or breasts automatically negate a woman's femaleness? Our sense of being 'female' or 'male' is surely more about self-identity than about biology. Essentially, however, the transsexual woman can never be 100% female; she can only approximate a change of sex. Hence, I call her a 'virtual woman'.

Some social theorists (see for example, West and Zimmerman, 1987; Butler, 1990; Ekins, 1996) view gender in terms of 'performance'. Indeed, Goffman sees the social world as a theatrical stage, with all of us 'performing' our social roles. Kessler and McKenna (1978) argue that the transsexual person has self-consciously to strive to 'do' their 'true' gender in a way that those of us who are not transsexual 'do naturally'. This is an interesting point, as it somewhat refutes other theorists' notions of the 'performance' or 'performativity' of gender, that it is something which we all *do*. The requirement of the Western psycho-medico professions for transsexuals to undergo a 'real life test' or 'real life experience' (as is discussed elsewhere in this book) as a prerequisite for the prescription of hormones and sex reassignment surgery indicates the need for transsexual people to study for and accomplish 'doing' female gender. This in itself conflicts with the convictions of many transsexual women who claim to have 'felt like a girl' from a very young age. If 'doing' gender comes 'naturally' the need for those who are transsexual to 'practice' (Kessler and McKenna, 1978) 'doing female' during transition would surely be unnecessary. Doctors, then, collude in the social construction of gender, in requiring that gender be 'performed' convincingly. While the 'drag artiste' (for example 'Lily Savage' or 'Dame Edna Everidge'), performs gender to a public audience, we tend to think of our own 'doing gender' as 'natural'. However, for some, to 'do' gender convincingly, gender has to be learnt.

In Harold Garfinkel's now classic ethno-methodological study of 'Agnes', a nineteen-year-old transsexual woman, he describes how Agnes had to learn how to 'do' gender in the female role. In order to achieve 'doing female', Agnes had to 'do' or accomplish certain things that represent the socially constructed notion of female gender 'performance'. Agnes strived to construct for herself the female gender role. Her boyfriend assumed the role of mentor, instructing Agnes in what he perceived as the 'correct' female role. Agnes welcomed her boyfriend's tutelage, indeed as Garfinkel reported, she had 'an abiding practical preoccupation with competent female sexuality' (Garfinkel, 1967, p.121). Agnes was convinced, and indeed managed to convince her medical practitioners as well as Garfinkel himself, that she was a female born in a male body, and that nature's 'mistake' should be corrected. She had reported that her breasts had developed spontaneously at puberty. The fact that these coexisted with her fully-grown male genitals did not dilute her femininity. Her performance of the female gender was so convincing that Agnes, a nineteen-year-old typist with only a basic educational background, was able to deceive her doctors and Garfinkel, only admitting, subsequent to her genital reassignment surgery, that she had been taking her mother's prescribed female hormone (contraception) pills since she was twelve years of age.

Sociologist Richard Ekins views transgendered women in terms of 'male-femaling', that is at once, 'deliberate', 'enacted', 'private' and 'public' (1997, p.35). *Doing* gender however, involves expressing our gender identity through a set of social rules and culturally defined norms. In society where there are but two genders: male and female, members of society are required, if they are to conform to the dominant cultural construction and meaning of gender, to fit into one or other of these two binary categories. For gender to conform to social and cultural norms and rules, we have to fit into what one could term a 'gender box', and if we do not fit, then we have to be modified so that we do. The transgender experience can be viewed in terms of 'gender migration' (King, 2004). Gender has its demarcation rules and those who dare to cross the securely guarded gender borders suffer social stigma (Goffman, 1963), ostracism and marginalisation. 'Male-femaling' takes on critical life events and life cycle crises, such as, for example, those of death or divorce, or any other separation. Indeed transitioning from male to female involves a *'petit mort'* or 'little death' or a separation from the former 'male' self and a 'rebirth' into the new female self. Transwomen gradually de-masculinize themselves, shedding, bit-by-bit, their maleness, to achieve (albeit 'virtual') womanhood. They do this by taking female hormones, by facial electrolysis and facial feminization surgery, breast augmentation surgery, and by learning how to socially perform as a woman. In short, they are trying to transform their fully-matured masculinity into a female form.

The symbolic interactionist (Blumer, 1969) perspective embraces the senses of self, identity and world that derive from social interaction with others. As members of society, then, individuals are social actors interacting within and 'inhabiting' social worlds (Ekins, 1997, p.18). One's cultural identity then comes down to a question of how one creates oneself. Gender problems reside within different spaces and times. History evolves and responses and attitudes to gender deviance alter with cultural changes that occur over time. 'Gender identity' then becomes the personal meaning we attach to our gendered selves within the context of the outer world, society, or culture. For Ekins, the concepts of 'self' and 'identity' are 'sensitizing concepts' (Ekins, 1997, p.18), therefore the 'social construction of human reality' (Weigart, 1983 cited in Ekins 1997, p.18) means that identity bestows upon the individual 'social meaning', whilst at the same time inhabiting the physical body.

4

Challenging the 'taken-for-granted'

The phenomenon called 'transsexualism' is one aspect of what Richard Ekins (1997) calls 'male-femaling'. For Ekins, 'male-femaling' challenges the social construction of 'gender role stereotypes'. For the 'conventional' person, gender is assigned at birth in accordance with the 'sexed' body. A male child is socialised as male, acts 'male' and is expected to grow up to be sexually attracted to females. A female child is socialised as such, acts 'female' and is expected to grow up to be sexually attracted to males (Ekins, 1997). All of these 'facts' can be accepted as 'taken-for-granted' 'truths'. For the transsexual person, this 'taken-for-grantedness' is problematic, as it inevitably causes them to question their senses of 'self' and 'identity' (Ekins, 1997, p.18). Transsexual people feel that they have been 'born into the wrong body' and typically experience their 'sexed' bodies and their gender identity as incongruent, and strive to fit into one or other of the two gender roles, constantly negotiating and renegotiating their transgendered embodiment. Questioning their gender identity, the transsexual woman's senses of 'self', 'identity' and indeed their 'worlds' have to be renegotiated. For the transsexual person, the meanings of 'self' and 'identity' are necessarily changing as they change sex. The social worlds of transsexuals revolutionize as they transition. Acting in the newly acquired female role facilitates for the transsexual woman, a new social world where, as she achieves virtual womanhood, her sense of self and identity are more integrated and whole (or holistic).

Sex categories as 'static' entities are socially constructed; however, when sex manifests itself as a transitory condition as in the case of transgender, the individual concerned experiences 'social stigma' or 'sexual stigma' (Plummer, 1975). Hence, it seems, the private body becomes the public property of the individual's culture and society, when any anomaly to the 'statistical average' of the social 'norm', is construed as deviant, irregular, and thus in need of remedy or cure. As anthropologist Mary Douglas theorised, in her now classic work, *Purity and Danger* (1966), dirt is not dirt, but simply 'matter out of place'. For Douglas, 'dirt' is that 'matter' which is situated outside of the permitted parameters of social order classification. Transgendered people are precariously placed on the parameters of accepted, ordered social classification of gender. This makes the transgendered person 'matter out of place' in a binary social order of gender. The transsexual woman cannot be fully integrated into 'womanhood'. She remains on the edges of womanhood, a 'virtual' woman.

I suggest that Western society views transsexual and transgendered individuals in Mary Douglas' theoretical perspective: each is viewed as an anomaly, or 'matter out of place' in a society that disallows 'otherness'. For Douglas, and for transsexual people, 'matter out of place' represents,

> ... uncomfortable facts, which refuse to be fitted in, we find ourselves ignoring or distorting so that they do not disturb these established assumptions (Douglas, 1966:49).

Transsexual women are keenly aware that they 'disturb established assumptions' and for this reason work hard to try and 'pass' as so-called 'natural' women, yet remaining Virtual Women.

For the male-to-female transsexual, once she has transitioned, 'passing' as a woman in society becomes a hiding strategy; the 'passing' person strives to blend into society, neatly fitting into a social structure that upholds the male-female gender divide and has no place for 'difference', variation or anomaly. The transsexual person feels that the only solution to the intense discomfort that they experience with their morphological body is to undergo hormone therapy and sex reassignment surgery to bring their body into line with their gender identity. In short, they undergo surgery in order to make the 'sexed' body match the 'brain sex', and to 'fit in' with the 'established assumptions' of gender that society makes.

Let us be clear at the outset, however, that a change of bodily sex can only be approximated. If we consider the situation: a transsexual woman has breasts that are artificially produced (by hormones or surgery) and an abdomen devoid of female reproductive organs. She retains some male biological characteristics, for example, the prostate gland is not removed during sex change surgery. Physical characteristics aside, however, it is also necessary to take account of social issues involved. But to quote reproductive biologist, Milton Diamond, 'Nature loves diversity; unfortunately, society does not'. Transgender is rarely socially accepted in society, as we shall discover.

6

Looking at gender variation

We can say that biology is the determining marker of the cultural and social ascription of gender. At birth, genitals are the essential insignia of gender, and in Western society, as I have already pointed out, there exists only two possible gender classifications: 'female' or 'male'. There are, however, anthropological examples in 'non-Western' societies that contradict the binary organisation of gender. Let us take a brief look at some gender variations in different cultures. In India, for example, we have the *Hijra*, known amongst themselves as the 'third gender' (see, for example, Nanda, 1993, 1999; Suthrell, 2004), and in traditional Native American culture the *Berdache* are not only accepted, but in many cases revered and in some cases even endowed with shamanic status (see Roscoe, 1993; Williams, 1986; Whitehead, 1981; Miller, J., 1982; Thayer, J.S., 1980; Hodes, M. (ed) 1999; Trexler, R. C. 1995). Cornwall (1994). Klein (1998); and Kulick (1996; 1998) have produced anthropological studies on Brazilian *Travesti* and accounts of the stigmatization of such transgendered prostitutes in Brazilian society. For an anthropological study of transgendering in the Philippines, see Johnson, M. (1997). Megan Sinnott (2004) highlights anthropological examples in Africa of 'female-female marriages' where an older, childless woman will marry a younger woman who will bear a child for her, fathered by a 'selected man' (Sinnott, 2004, p.41). Sinnott further notes the ubiquitous female *Berdache* of traditional Native American culture, who 'expressed a proclivity toward masculine-defined activities', including 'socially sanctioned marriage to woman' (Sinnott, 2004, p.41).

Scholars researching transgender in various cultures and societies around the world have drawn attention to the marginalization and discrimination that these groups have experienced (see Kulick, 1998; Nanda, 1993; 1999; Suthrell, 2004). In Western society, discrimination of transsexual persons stems in part from the early classification of the phenomenon as a 'mental' or 'psychological' disorder, and this in turn translates into the stigmatization of those citizens who fall outside of the social 'norm'. Certainly there has been a proliferation of medical discourse surrounding transsexuals and transgender, and the classification of gender dysphoria or transsexualism as a psychological disorder has resulted in transsexual people being denied their civil rights (Whittle, 2002). Instead of treating the phenomenon as a variation in human diversity, it is psycho-pathologized as some kind of mental disorder and thus stigmatized. Indeed, in the International Classification of Diseases (ICD-10) and 1980 version of the American Diagnostic and Statistical Manual (DSMIIIR), transsexuality is classed as a mental disorder and one that should be 'treated' by psychiatrists (Whittle, 2002). Subsequently the DSMIV (1994) replaced the classification 'transsexual' with 'gender identity disorder'. In 1975 the removal of 'homosexuality' from DSMIII coincided with 'Gender Identity Disorder' being included as a 'medical disorder' in that volume (Whittle, 2002). However, as Whittle argues (as do some of the transsexual women of this study; see for example, Nicole's story later in this book) the medical and psychiatric establishments should (as Whittle maintains) take a 'diagnostic' and 'enabling' role (Whittle, 2002, p.72), rather than that of gatekeeper. As noted above, the classification of transsexualism as a medical or psychiatric 'disorder' serves to further stigmatize those whose gender identity falls outside of the binary paradigm of gender classification.

When sex and gender identities fall outside of the categories of 'male' and 'female', this challenges certain 'Western'[1] conventional taken-for-granted assumptions that there are only two sexes, and causes chaos with belief systems and social mores. This book explores the social and personal worlds of those people who fall in that social space that anthropologist Victor Turner calls, *betwixt and between* (Turner, V. 1970, p.97). I see the transgendered as 'betwixt and between' in gender, as they fall outside of the bipolar model of male-female with its distinct, immutable and exclusive gender categories.

---

1   In this book I refer to the 'West' or 'Western' as those geographical areas that include not only England but also North America, and western, southern and northern Europe. In this sense, Said (1978/1995) distinguishes the West as occidental and the East (or orient) as oriental. Although my cross-cultural comparative analysis of transgender is concerned specifically with England and Thailand, there are times when it is more relevant to include the West as a population in general, rather than a specific western population, i.e. England.

Some ideas on the 'causes' of transsexualism

In Western society gender emphasis is on genitals at birth. Our sex — male or female — is assumed at birth based upon a cursory glance at the genitals, the essential insignia of sex classification. It is also assumed that 'gender identity' will automatically align with 'biological sex', and that these are congruent. In contemporary Western societies, those people who do not experience this harmony between physical, biological, anatomical sex and gender identity, experience incongruity and the overwhelming inner knowing that their 'sexed' bodies do not match their gendered minds. There is now a growing proliferation of medical and scientific research that suggests gender identity is located 'in the brain' and that the phenomenon called 'transsexualism' could have a neurobiological origin (see for example, Kruijver, 2004; Diamond, 2000; Zhou, et al, 1995). This makes perfect sense; for otherwise, the drive to change the body to match the mind and all that such a process entails, would not be so forceful.

Tracing the transgender phenomenon ...

As far back as Ancient Greece, physician Hippocrates (460-377 BC) and philosopher, Aristotle (384-322 BC), were claiming that sex differentiation takes place in the brain. Around a century ago, scientists' interest in sex differentiation in the brain led them to study morphological and weight differences in human male and female brains. By the mid-twentieth century, according to Krujver (2004, p.7), scientists had reasoned that *'... if testosterone was critical to the masculine differentiation of genitalia ...'* then it naturally followed that *'... it might also be important in the differentiation of the brain'*. Half a century on, in 2000, scientists in the Netherlands reported that sex differences found in *'Somatostatin neuronal sex differences in the bed nucleus of the stria terminalis (BSTc)'* strongly suggested that in transsexuals sex differentiation of the brain and genitals *'... may go in opposite directions'* and that this knowledge pointed to a *'neurological basis of gender identity disorder'* (Kruijver, 2004, p.28).

Neuroscientist Frank Kruijver of the Institute for Brain Research in the Netherlands claims that *'Sexual differentiation is a sequential process which starts from the moment of conception* [and] *... sex chromosomes*

determine genetic sex ... and [then] *the gonadal sex'*, and this in turn '...
determines the developing brain sex...' (2004, p.7). Indeed, as reproductive
biologist, Milton Diamond states, gender identity is located not in
the genitals, but 'between the ears' (Diamond, 1982; 2000; personal
communication in conversation with Diamond, 2003). However, such
scientific epistemologies contradict and to some extent clash with a social
constructionist view of gender and the 'performativity' or 'performance'
of gender proffered by some theorists. Moreover, while transsexualism is
noted in volumes of Diagnostic and Statistical Manual (DSMIIIR, 1980;
DSMIV, 1994) and ICD-10 (International Classification of Diseases)
as not being a psychiatric condition, it is nonetheless 'treated' as such
by the psychiatric and medical establishments.

A transsexual child, born with an apparently male body, will experience
confusion because it is automatically assumed by parents, teachers and
others that 'he' will take an interest in "boys' toys" and games but
will actually prefer to play "girls' games". In this way, performativity of
gender is out of kilter and this can lead to a deep and intense sense of
discomfort and a dialectic between the self-identity that comes from an
'inner knowing' of who (s)he is and the social and gendered role (s)he
is expected to perform. 'Opposite' gendered behaviour often manifests
in the form of a strong urge to 'cross-dress' and for the transsexual child,
this would take the form of secretly dressing in his sister's or his mother's
clothes. This book examines the social problems that are encountered by
transsexual women in British culture and society as compared to those
experienced by *kathoey* in Thai culture and society. The book examines
the phenomenon that is called 'transsexualism' or 'transgenderism' and
investigates the protracted and problematic transitioning process that the
English participants of this study experience as compared to the more
easily facilitated process that exists for *kathoey* in Thailand. Although
transsexualism is not a mental illness, such a person is described in
Western medico-psychiatric terms as suffering from 'Gender Dysphoria'
(International Classification of Diseases (ICD-10, 1992); DSMIIIR,
1980; DSMIV, 1994) or 'Gender Identity *Disorder*' (my emphasis).
Such terms assume that the phenomenon is some kind of 'mental' or
'psychological' condition, which serve to pathologize the phenomenon

as some kind of deviance, rather than accept and understand it as one more variety of human experience. Some non-Western societies celebrate a 'third gender' category as just one more aspect of human diversity that coexists within a vast multicoloured rainbow of possibilities. The case of the Thai *kathoey* illustrates this. The stories of the transwomen in this book suggest that dealing with transsexualism in Western society can cause a great deal of emotional distress to the person themselves, and to their families, spouses and significant others. In contrast, the transgender phenomenon in Thailand, though not by any means unproblematic, is, in some senses, celebrated as part of humanity's rich diversity.

So — what is 'a transsexual'?

> *Who is a transsexual?*
> *Anyone whose performance of gender calls into question*
> *the construct of gender itself.*
> (Bornstein, 1994:121)

It seems to me that the human desire to express one's gender identity is a powerful one and the person denied the freedom of such expression of their gender identity suffers considerable mental and emotional strife. We have established that the term 'transsexual' refers to a person who desires to live or actually does live full-time in the 'opposite' gender role. The desire to change gender is overwhelming to the point that in some cases, the person feels that they have to either transition or die; such is the depth of their despair and emotional conflict. However, we need to remember to distinguish the 'transsexual' from other categories of the transgender phenomenon. As stated, the term 'male-to-female transsexual' refers to a person who is born apparently male with unambiguous genitalia, but from a very early age feels him/herself to be female.

I seek to interpret the transgender experience from the point of view of the virtual women themselves. While *kathoey* were less interested in conjecture as to why they are *kathoey* (beyond the Buddhist belief that their *kathoey* status was a paying back of 'karmic debt'; more on Buddhism later) for the participants from England, this issue was crucial to them. Most, if not all, were aggrieved that a 'medical condition' that they believed they were born with had so negatively affected their lives as social actors and denied them the opportunity to freely express their 'true' gender identity.

The starting point of this book, then, derives from the neurobiological thesis that in some individuals 'brain sex' is at odds with 'biological' sex, and that this phenomenon, variously called 'transsexualism', 'transsexuality', 'gender identity disorder' or 'gender dysphoria' brings with it personal anxiety and emotional problems for the individual concerned as well as their families, significant 'others', and indeed, society at large. This is because transgender in conventional Western society upsets the social order of classificatory systems; it represents a foot in each gender camp, an abomination of the 'natural' order of humanity. Transsexual women — those who fall 'betwixt and between' genders — also disallow the maintenance of social order by disrupting taken-for-granted assumptions of the binary gendered classifications of male-female. From the point of view of the British Virtual Women of my research study, however, psychiatric evaluation and 'treatment' by the psychiatric profession is highly inappropriate, especially in light of the 'neuroscientific' suggestions reported by Kruijver (2004). In the very different culture of Thailand (and, indeed, some other non-Western societies), however, the transgender phenomenon represents not a gender deviance, but yet another aspect of humanity's rich diversity and there seems to be little or no concern over whether it has biological origins or not. Intriguingly, it is the assumption of the British virtual women featured in this book that transsexualism is 'innate' and therefore present at birth and that gender identity is fixed. This paradigm sits in diametric opposition to any theory that might suppose that gender identity is plastic and malleable and subject to change; in short, that nurture can conquer nature. But can it?

The gender experiment that went wrong

Assuming that the scientific theory of a neurobiological basis is sound, we can accept that transsexualism is 'innate' and therefore present at birth and that gender identity is fixed. This paradigm sits in diametric opposition to any theory that gender identity is plastic and malleable and subject to change; in short, that nurture can conquer nature. American psychologist John Money experimented with the notion of the plasticity of gender identity in his now (in)famous study of identical twin boys. He was motivated to demonstrate that as human beings we possess flexibility in our psychosocial identity. In Canada in 1966, the young mother of seven month old identical twins, Bruce and Brian Reimer, left her babies in a hospital to undergo circumcision to correct a urination problem that both boys were experiencing. Bruce was the first twin to be operated upon, and the procedure involved cauterization of the foreskin. By a tragic accident the baby's penis was burned and totally ablated.[2] After some months of extreme anxiety, the distraught parents sought the help of John Money, psychologist at the Johns Hopkins University Gender Identity Clinic in Baltimore. Drawing on his theory of an infant's gender 'neutrality'[3] for the first two years of life, that starts from the premise that 'nurture' carries more weight than 'nature', Money immediately advised gender reassignment by the amputation of the testes and the scrotal sac used in a surgical procedure to fashion a rudimentary vulva, (which took place when the baby was 17 months of age) and to thereafter raise the boy as a girl. He also counselled the parents never to let the child know 'she' was ever a boy (*Horizon*, BBC2 television, 4 November 2004). The baby's name was changed from Bruce to Brenda and 'she' became the subject of Money's experiment to 'prove' that gender identity is 'learnt behaviour' and easily moulded or remodelled, with the other twin, Brian, being used as the 'control' subject. Money reported that he had counselled the parents on the *'... future prognosis and management of their "new daughter"',* assuring them that they could expect the child to *'... differentiate a female gender identity'* in accordance with her 'sex of rearing' (Money 1975, p.67).

---

2 After the accident, the second twin, Brian, was left uncircumcised, and by some tragic irony his problem with urination corrected itself.

3 Speaking on the *Horizon* documentary film, *"The Boy with no penis"* (BBC2, 4 November 2004), Professor Richard Green, consultant psychiatrist at the Charing Cross Hospital Gender Identity Clinic in London, upheld the 'gender neutrality at birth' theory espoused by Money.

Both twins were regularly seen on an annual basis by Money, who proceeded to publish a book (*Man and woman/Boy and girl*, Money, J. & Ehrhardt, A.A. 1972) and articles for the scientific community declaring the 'experiment' as a huge success that 'proved' that nurture triumphed over nature when it comes to gender identity and psychosocial or psychosexual adjustment, and that gender identity was not something that was fixed at birth. Indeed, he was later to claim with confidence,

> *Now 9 years old, she has differentiated a female gender identity in marked contrast to the male gender identity of her brother* (Money 1975, p.66)

And this led to his belief that,

> *... gender identity is sufficiently incompletely differentiated at birth as to permit successful assignment of a genetic male as a girl. Gender identity then differentiates in keeping with the experiences of rearing.* (Money, 1975, p.67)

In conclusion, Money claimed of 'Brenda',

> *Her behavior is so normally that of an active little girl, and so clearly different by contrast from the boyish ways of her twin brother, that it offers nothing to stimulate one's conjectures.* (Money, 1975, p.71).

However, whilst Money basked in his pseudo-scientific glory, Brenda's life and that of her family was fraught with conflict and difficulty. 'Brenda', (who as an adolescent became 'David' of his own volition), was later to report that he had never been comfortable as a girl (recall, the child had never been made aware that 'she' had been born male), and that he rejected his 'girl's' toys in favour of his brother's more masculine toys[4]. By the time 'Brenda' reached adolescence, the conflict she experienced with her gender identity was so great that she refused to go to Baltimore for any more

---

4 *Horizon* documentary film, *"The boy with no penis"*, BBC2, 4 November 2004

consultations with John Money ('she' was later to describe the sessions with Money as 'abusive' (Colapinto, 2000))[5], who subsequently reported that she had been 'lost to follow-up'. In the meantime, reproductive biologist, Milton Diamond, who had doubted Money's findings throughout, set about tracking down Brenda and her family. It took him twelve years and when he did meet 'Brenda' (who was by now aged in his mid-thirties and living as a man having changed his name to David) he unearthed the truth about Money's claims of the 'success' of his 'nurture overriding nature' experiments. Henceforth, the case was referred to as the 'John/Joan' study.

Notwithstanding John Money's failed 'John/Joan' experiment in fact succeeds in one ironic, yet crucial respect: *the transsexual person seeking gender reassignment typically reports having felt themselves, from a very early age, to be of their opposite somatic gender* (interviews). The fact that neither hormone nor psychiatric treatment, nor indeed 'female' social conditioning could turn the 'John/Joan' twin into a girl teaches us more about the complexities of psychosocial conditioning and gender identity than did Money's intended experiment findings. While Money set about demonstrating the flexibility of human psychosexual identity, what his work does suggest very strongly is, incontrovertibly, the opposite: that no amount of hormone therapy or psychological conditioning can change a person's gender identity, which is, one would conclude, seemingly 'fixed' at birth. It is noteworthy that Richard Green (1999), who had been an advocate of Money's work at the time of the 'John/Joan' experiment, has more recently conceded that,

> *... severe gender dysphoria cannot be alleviated by any conventional psychiatric treatment. This is true whether treatment be psycho-analytic, eclectic, aversion treatment, or by any standard psychiatric drugs ...* (Green, R. (1999) cited in GIRES (2004))

And David? In 2004, he committed suicide; his twin brother, Brian, had taken his own life two years earlier.

---

5 Green concluded that Money's decision to reassign the baby's gender 'was the correct one' at the time.

CHAPTER TWO
Gender Migration and Rites of Passage

'Gender Migration'

For sociologist, Dave King 'sex-changing' is, from a sociological perspective, most usefully viewed as 'gender migration' (2003, pp.173-194). In my view, individuals who 'migrate' from one side of the socially constructed gender binary to the other, to some extent collude in the maintenance of an exclusively male-female bipolar gender set-up. I agree with King, however, that gender migrants, like geographical migrants, face conflicts that render them socially marginalized:

> *Migrants of both kinds are regarded as undesirable and threatening; the legitimacy of settlement in the new country/ gender may be denied; the granting of citizenship and other rights may be refused* ... (King, 2003, p.173).

The geographical migrant is frequently required to obtain a visa to allow them entry into another country. In England, transsexual individuals now have the right to such a 'visa' under the terms of the Gender Recognition Act (2004) (known as the GRA) in the form of a Gender Recognition Certificate (known as then GRC) that legally recognises their new gender status. (In Thailand, however, *kathoey* are allowed no such 'visa', meaning that they remain male under Thai law — more on this in the next chapter!).

Once across the gender border, the transsexual person, then, has to 'create a new pattern of reality' (see Mary Douglas, 1966, p.51). Like the geographical migrant, the gender migrant (King, 2003) seeks a new life, rendered possible through hormone therapy and sex reassignment surgery, but as I will illustrate, such a new life is, somewhat inevitably, achieved by compromise. The exchange of the original gendered body, an 'alien' body, that which they feel does not belong to them, for a new one, the 'correct' body, the rightful physicality that they feel was mistakenly denied them at birth, is now a viable proposition in the age of advanced surgical technology.

Rituals of gender passage

The gender migrant, not unlike the geographical migrant, once the gender borders have been crossed (post-surgically) faces a period of integration in the new gender role. However, this is a stage that is reached via the long transitional journey that is travelled and that starts from the first realisation that the gender identity conflict from which they suffer is a 'medically recognised' condition that is 'treatable' with hormones and surgery. This journey, as discussed below, is traversed via a liminal period, within which they are, quite literally, 'betwixt and between' in gender. It seems to me that there is an analogous link between what Anthropologist Arnold van Gennep calls in his now classic works, 'territorial passages' and 'frontiers', and the feminist boundaries (see, for example, Raymond, 1979[6]) that seek to exclude transsexual women from the 'natural' world of women, or a 'prohibition against entering a given territory ...' (1908/1977, p.16). In her autobiography, Deirdre McCloskey (1999), who migrated from male to female, refers to her transition as 'crossing', inferring that some kind of 'gender border' or 'territorial passage' had to be crossed in order to take her out from the male and into the female domain at the 'frontiers' of gender classification. It is the keepers of these 'frontiers' or feminist boundaries that seek to exclude transsexual women from the gender camp of 'real' women, where a 'prohibition against entering a given territory' (van Gennep, 1908/1977, p.16) in a 'system of zones' (van Gennep, 1908/1977, p.18) operates and renders the transsexual person in a state of flux. As Arnold van Gennep's thesis illustrates,

> ... *whoever passes from one [zone] to the other finds himself [sic] physically ... in a special situation for a certain length of time; he [sic] wavers between two worlds ... (1908/1977, p.18).*

---

6 In her 1979 book, *The Transsexual Empire* ... feminist Janice Raymond's polemical arguments are correct in some aspects of her postulates. Transsexuals in North America and Western Europe are dealt with under the patriarchal psycho-medical establishment; its practitioners are (commonly) men. Raymond properly refers to Money, Green and Stoller as the 'trinity of men' who 'dominate the field' when it comes to the treatment of patients with gender identity problems. At the time of writing, Green works as one of the principle practitioners dealing with British transsexual patients at a Gender Identity Clinic in the UK.

Anne Bolin (1988, p.69) discusses the ways in which the transsexual participants of her study *'... were participants in a rite of passage that dramatized their movement from one status to another ...'.* 'Becoming' a woman involves for transsexuals *'... the transmutation of the personal identity ...'.* As such, transsexual women have reported experiencing a 'wavering'[7] between two genders (interviews) as they try to 'fit in' the 'natural' world of women. Indeed, for McCloskey (1999, p.176), being accepted into the female realm is achieved, not just by surgery, but rather, as she states, *'You become a woman by being treated as one of the tribe'* indicating that, as the narratives of the Virtual Women of this study will illustrate, there is more to being accepted as a woman than merely the outward results of hormone treatment and sex reassignment and related surgeries. Indeed, one psychiatrist interviewed for this study reported on a patient of his who bypassed the NHS route and travelled to Thailand for sex reassignment surgery and other 'feminizing' surgeries, only to regret transitioning. He told me that his patient is now back in England, and *'... shelling out thousands to have as much reversed as possible ... it takes more than just how you look'.* As Simone de Beauvoir has theorised, we are not born women, but 'become' women (de Beauvoir, 1949[8]). For sure, to claim that one is 'born a woman' would be a physiological nonsense. A female child 'becomes' a woman via social conditioning and biological, emotional and intellectual maturation. A transsexual person in British society 'becomes', if not a biological, then a 'social' woman through the protracted journey of transition, and rites of passage, those events marked by various stages and noted by Arnold van Gennep, when he wrote so long ago of cultures that mark stages of maturation by customs of ritual: *'rites de passage'* (van Gennep, 1908/1977; see also Bolin, 1988; 1993). Arnold van Gennep studied the *rites de passage* through which people journey at various stages in their lives and the rituals pertaining thereto. Analogously, the transitioning transsexual person undergoes such rites of passage on the journey that takes them across the gendered borders

---

7   Ekins and King (1996) use the term 'oscillating' to describe individuals who waver between male and female genders.

8 Butler (1990) also discusses de Beauvoir's thesis on this issue.

prevailing in society. Another anthropologist, Victor Turner (1967, p.94) regarded transition as '... *a process, a becoming, and in the case of rites de passage, even a transformation ...'*. For van Gennep, (cited by Turner, 1967, p.94) rites of passage are defined as, *'... rites, which accompany ... change of place, state, social position and age ...'*

Indeed, van Gennep viewed rites of passage as made up of three phases: separation, margin (liminality) and aggregation. The initial phase involves the separation or detachment of the individual from their *'earlier fixed point in the social structure'* (van Gennep in Turner, 1967, p.94). For the transsexual women of this study, this first phase also involves a separation; that is, separation or detachment or shedding even, of the old 'male' self, as the individual embarks upon the transition from male to female. Like the snake shedding its skin (Turner, 1967, p.99), the person inside is the same person as before, but the new outer physicality (or 'skin') is transformed into the new 'female' body; a process akin to that of metamorphosis. The second phase of van Gennep's rites of transition involves a period of liminality, the intervening period when the individual is quite literally, as Victor Turner called it, 'betwixt and between'. The status of the individual in this phase of *rite de passage* is ambiguous as they traverse through a place, or a state of being, that is almost devoid of or has only few of the features of either their past or previous state and the new 'becoming' state (Turner, 1967, p.94). Likewise, for the transsexual women of this study, this liminal stage involves existing in a space between genders. The transgender 'passenger' in this phase has as yet no legitimate place in either of the gender binary spaces; (s)he has begun the voyage from male to female, but although (s)he has left the point of embarkation, (s)he has not yet completed the 'gender migration' journey. The African Ndembu society studied by Victor Turner has no definition for neophytes with 'not-boy-not-man' status, and similarly, British society has no such status for the transsexual woman, (the 'transitional being') undergoing transition from male-to-female. (S)he is 'not-man-not-woman'. Such persons are, as Turner would put it,

> *... neither one thing nor another; or may be both; or neither*
> *here nor there; or may even be nowhere ... (1967, p.97).*

Indeed, for Turner, transitional beings, '*... are at once no longer classified and not yet classified*' (1967, p.96). In other words, such beings are unseen, what Turner (1967, p.96) terms, the 'structural invisibility' of liminality or 'structurally dead' as far as a society's constructs are concerned. So too, is the transitioning transsexual woman in British society; as a 'male' she exists no longer, yet as a 'woman' she is yet to be 'born' or constructed. Moreover, like Turner's Ndembu neophyte, modern society has no legitimate classification for the transitioning transsexual woman. Therefore, she is, as stated, 'betwixt and between' in gender. Even when they have fully transitioned and are living full time in the female gender role, such individuals are, to use my own term, '*Virtual*' women. They can never fully inhabit the female world, but dwell just inside the borders, no longer male, but not fully female either. Turner states that the neophytes of his study were regarded as, indeed likened to, 'newborn infants', and it is of some significance that a number of the transsexual women of my study described to me their transition from male to female as being 'reborn'. (Indeed, one informant believed that she was the reincarnation of her mother's baby daughter who had died in infancy before she (the transsexual) was born. Yet another informant simply stated, '*It's out with the old and in with the new*'.) It is noteworthy that for Turner's neophytes, gender according to a bipolar paradigm does not exist. They are regarded as being (like the transitioning transsexual, and indeed the *kathoey* or 'third sex'), neither male nor female, or are assigned, symbolically, features of both genders, regardless of their natal sex (Turner, 1967, p.98).

The third and final stage of the 'passage' is the consummation. Here the individual, states Turner,

> *... is in a stable state once more and ... has rights and*
> *obligations of a clearly defined ... type, and is expected*
> *to behave in accordance with certain customary norms ...*
> *(1967, p.94).*

Here, I have discussed King's notion of 'gender migration' and the rituals that transsexual people necessarily have to undergo in order to undertake the transitional journey, relating these to van Gennep's *rites de passage* and Turner's thesis on transitioning and the liminal period. Now let us consider transsexual women as they reach their gender destination and try to assimilate themselves into their new (or 'true') gender.

Arrival at the gender destination

For the transsexual 'passenger' once she has reached her gender destination, her consummation in her new gender role requires a social invisibility; her previous gender has to be 'hidden'[9] in a society that has a bipolar gender classification, and where there may be no legitimate place for 'gender migrants'. Further, the fully transitioned transsexual woman has to decide whether to covertly take on and fulfil the social requirements pertaining to the female gender, as she assimilates herself into society, 'passing' as a woman, or alternatively, to overtly self-identify as a 'transsexual' woman (as opposed to a 'woman'), whilst still living, as far as possible, 'in role'. At the same time, however, by conforming to a binary paradigm of gender, transsexual people uphold the notion that humans can only be male or female, with nothing in between.

For the British transsexual women of my study, van Gennep's phase two may continue through and to some extent, replace phase three. Integration into the 'new' gender is attempted through what sociologist Erving Goffman calls 'passing', the passing person blending into society, their previous identity invisible to others. (In contrast, *kathoey* are highly visible and recognizable on the streets of Thailand.) In this way, reference points to their previous gender are minimized or eliminated as they endeavour to reach a point of integration. However, like geographical migrants, there is always the possibility of ending up unassimilated, as a person dwelling on the margins or a person in a marginal group, for as McCloskey claims, *It's hard to pass ... you just try it'* (1999, p.160).

---

9   Challenging Janice Raymond's castigation of transgender/transsexual 'males', Sandy Stone (1996:295) argues, *'It is difficult to generate a counter-discourse if one is programmed to disappear'.*

One of the reasons that 'passing' is, as McCloskey maintains, 'hard' is because typically the Western transsexual woman is middle aged or older before she begins her transition, hence necessitating the need to try and transform a fully masculinized body into a female form. This is mainly due to the fact that transgender in Western societies tends to carry with it huge social stigma and for this reason, in contrast to the *kathoey* child in Thailand, the child suffering from gender dysphoria in Western society internalizes and keeps secret the knowledge of the incongruence they experience between their gender identity and physical body. Subsequently, the British transwomen of my study reported having felt compelled to keep their transsexual status under wraps, and closeted for fear of rejection by family, friends, employers and society at large. Further, once the person has acknowledged and revealed their transsexual status, the transitioning process can take several years and even then in England, sex reassignment surgery on the NHS is not guaranteed.

We will look more closely at the transitioning process, through the voices of the transsexual women themselves, in later chapters. But for now, let me take you to Thailand and the world of the Thai *kathoey*...

CHAPTER THREE
Kathoey ◆ The Third Sex
Thailand's Ladyboys

What is a '*kathoey*'?

> '*Kathoey — that ubiquitous but enigmatic subculture*'
> (Totman, 2003, p.61)

A *kathoey* (also known as a 'Ladyboy' by Thai speakers of English) can simply be described as a person who is born into an unambiguously male body, and as such, raised as a boy but at a relatively early age, the *kathoey* expresses their gender in terms of the female social role. *Kathoey* are also regarded as '*poo-ying praphet sorng*' (a 'second kind of woman') or '*sao praphet sorng*' (a 'second kind of girl'). In Thai folklore terms, the *kathoey* is also viewed as a 'fruitless' or 'infertile' tree or plant (I am grateful to Oradol Panbhat, 2006 for this explanation; see also Sinnott, 2004). In Thailand, *kathoey* can be found in all walks of life and occupations throughout the country, but are notably represented in the sex industry, as well as in cabaret shows catering to tourists and Thais alike.

The existing literature on *kathoey* and their history in Siamese/Thai culture is scant and one reason for this is likely due to the fact that until the twentieth century only Thai monks and the 'nobility' were able to read and write. However, monks, academics (that is, the few who write on transgender in Thailand) and Thais in general agree that *kathoey* have formed an integral and indigenous part of 'Thai' culture for hundreds of years (Totman, 2003, p.64). In 1995, scholar of Thai studies, Peter Jackson (1995, pp.192-3) argued that, historically, there seems to have been a designated cultural role for *kathoey*. However, in a later paper (2003) Jackson concedes that he may have misjudged this concept. To help us understand the transgender phenomenon in Thailand, let us take a look at the predominant religion of the country: Buddhism.

Buddhism and the 'third sex'

Buddhism is the overwhelmingly predominant 'religion' in Thailand. Approximately 95% of the Thai population is Buddhist (Totman, 2003, p.47). However, Buddhism is perhaps more appropriately defined, not as a 'religion' but as a philosophy, a way of life, or a way of 'being'. Buddhist monks live by a clerical code of conduct, called *'Vinaya'* (Jackson, 1996). *Vinaya* identifies not two, but four main sex and gender types: male, female, and two more called *'ubhatobyanjanaka'* and *'pandaka'* (Jackson, 1996; Totman, 2003, p.51) and these are defined differently in different parts of the Pali canon[10], so we need to make these distinctions. *Ubhatobyanjanaka* suggests the concept of hermaphroditism. In Pali, the root word *'ubhato'* means 'two-fold'; *'byanjanaka'* means a sign of gender; hence *ubhatobyanjanaka* refers to persons who display the signs of both male and female genders. Bunmi Methangkun (1986 cited in Jackson, 1996) draws our attention to the notion that there are psychological as well as physical characteristics of both sexes and genders. Therefore, looking at this category we need to recognise that they display both psychological and biological characteristics as well as those male or female characteristics that are culturally ascribed (Jackson, 1996). *Pandaka,* on the other hand, describes the gendered body in terms of deficiency, rather than, as with *ubhatobyanjanaka,* a term that describes the gendered body in terms of biological and psychological attributes. The term *'Pandaka'* seems to have evolved into a category that includes 'non-normative male sexuality' (Jackson, 1996). Further, Peter Jackson suggests that the word *'Pandaka'* may be derived from *'anda';* the Pali meaning of which is 'egg' or 'testicle' and this may denote 'male reproductive deficiency or incapacity' (Jackson, 1996). Confusingly, there are five different types of *Pandaka,* however, *kathoey* is unrelated to two of them. Jackson also suggests that even though the term *'kathoey'* (originating, probably, from Khmer) is commonly used as the translation of 'Pandaka', none of the five sub-categories of *'Pandaka'* describes cross-gender behaviour.

---

10 Pali is an ancient Indo-European language derived from Sanskrit and formerly spoken in parts of India.

'Karma' and kathoey

Buddhism's most characteristic feature is the belief in *Karma, Karmic law* or *Karmic debt*. Karma describes a life not as that which begins at birth and ends in death, but rather as a continuum, or a chain of events that link 'past life' with 'present life' with 'future life'. Under karmic law, all actions have a cause and an effect, and this places the responsibility for all actions, whether 'good' or 'bad' squarely at the door of the individual themselves. Furthermore, the Buddhist philosophy recognises that as individuals we can be 're-born' or reincarnated in any of three sex categories: female, male or *kathoey* (Jackson, 1995; Allyn, 2002). In Thai Buddhist philosophy, the sex category '*kathoey*' is predetermined, as indeed are the sex categories of female and male. To accept that sex category is predetermined allows for and leads to an acceptance of that which is not possible to change. As Sinnott (2004, p.104) notes, '*... to postulate choice suggests that change is possible and perhaps desirable. To postulate 'born-to-be' negates any suggestion of change and calls for acceptance of what cannot be altered ...*'

It is perhaps for this reason, that *kathoey* status is not regarded as negatively in Thailand as is transgender in the more Judeo-Christian traditions predominant in the Western hemisphere. Buddhism then, and a recognised paradigm of at least three gender categories, female/male/ *kathoey* (or 'third sex') perhaps play a part in the generally neutral, if not exactly positive, attitude to transgender that exists in Thai society, and the resultant more facilitative opportunity for *kathoey* to openly express their gender identity. However, such a philosophy also prohibits or denies the individual any sense of personal choice or 'agency', or the 'right' to make personal decisions about one's sex or gender, as Sinnott notes.

Whereas *kathoey* 'suffer' karmically, in terms of taking on the female gender role, paradoxically, they enjoy a kind of freedom that Thai society denies to normative-gender Thai women. However, it would be a distortion of the truth to hold up Thai culture and society as unflinchingly tolerant of *kathoey*. While *kathoey* in some aspects are generally socially accepted, in Thai society this acceptance depends upon context. For example, for a *kathoey*, a university degree in no way guarantees graduate level employment. It is by no means unusual for *kathoey* to graduate from university and end up working in low-level jobs or as *kathoey* cabaret dancers, subsidising their income by sex work. More crucially, *kathoey* remain legally 'male' and are classified as such for life.

However, on the face of it and in contrast to Western society in general, *kathoey* enjoy freedom of transgender expression in ways that elude their transsexual sisters in England. The reason for this may be linked to the aforementioned Buddhist laws of karma, and the principle of cause and effect. Some interpret '*kathoey*' as a gender status in terms of the repayment of a karmic debt. The Buddhist philosophy embraces five precepts (see for example, Allyn, 2002) that apply to lay people[11], the third of which is an admonition to refrain from sexual misconduct. Interpretation of this third precept, regards sexual misconduct as including adultery, as does rape and the sexual abuse of children. *Kathoey* are believed to be repaying karmic debt, having been, in a previous life, for example, a man who may have committed adultery or abandoned a woman whom he had impregnated (I learned this from conversations with *kathoey* in Chiang Mai, 2003; also, see for example, Jackson 1995; Matzner, 2004; Totman, 2003). In general then, Thai society's attitude to *kathoey* derives from the philosophy that they are to be 'pitied' as beings who 'suffer' in this life because they are merely repaying karmic debt accrued as a result of past life transgression. In other words, it could happen to anyone.

The relationship between Buddhist monks and women is hierarchically unbalanced in Thailand, and this can also affect *kathoey*. For example, a woman is not permitted to physically touch a monk, nor can she hand directly to a monk any object. To hand an object to a monk, a woman must either pass it via a male third party, or place it on a table covered by a silk cloth that a monk has placed upon it. I observed this phenomenon on several occasions on domestic flights in Thailand. The monk would sit in the window seat, with his male companion in the aisle seat. The female flight attendant would pass refreshments to the man in the aisle seat, who in turn would pass this to the monk. This cultural tradition raised for me some questions regarding the relationship between monks and *kathoey*. For example, can a pre-operative *kathoey* touch a monk? What if such a

---

11 Monks have 227 precepts, while novice monks have ten, and nuns have eight precepts (Allyn, 2002).

kathoey were dressed in female attire is she then a 'woman' or still 'male', (as indeed she remains under Thai law)? Likewise, what of the post-op *kathoey*; does she retain her 'male' status in this regard, as she does her legal status as a male? However, seeking information proved in itself problematic. Significantly, there seems to be a dearth of sociological material addressing this issue, indeed, I found none at all. My second plan of action was to approach various scholars of Thai/transgender studies for advice, but to no avail. Finally, I enquired of two *kathoey* friends as to the relationship dynamics involving *kathoey* and monks. It seems that the Thai cultural condition that prioritizes 'appearances' over all, and proscribes 'loss of face' extends to the *kathoey* relationship with the Buddhist monk. Following my enquiry, the first *kathoey*, a post-op transsexual woman reported that (and I translate her words here),

> *After I had the operation [sex reassignment surgery] to be a lady my outwardly appearance is as same as the real woman. So, I'm not allowed to touch the Buddhist monk; because if Thais should see that it could cause great problems.*

My second informant in this regard, a pre-operative *kathoey*, reported that so long as the *kathoey* presented as 'male', there should be no problem with her touching a monk, and this was because in Thai culture, 'appearances are everything'. Intriguingly, Thai Buddhist monks, who live a life of celibacy, and whom women, including their own mothers are not permitted to touch, are regarded as a 'neutral' or 'third' sex.

The practice of the Buddhist philosophy that is such an integral part of Thai life may be one explanation as to why *kathoey*, wanting to feminize their bodies, do not have to negotiate the strict regime upheld by the psycho-medico professions as experienced by transsexuals in England. For example, criteria for sex reassignment surgery performed on Thai transsexuals do not routinely include lengthy psychiatric or psychological evaluation.[12] One reason for this may lie in the basic traditions of Thai culture and society of family members and friends who ordinarily rely

---

12 Thai surgeons I interviewed reported that they sometimes require *kathoey* to undergo psychiatric evaluation if or when they suspect a 'psychosis'.

on each other for cross-generational and inter-generational emotional support as well as for financial and practical needs. In Thailand, where there exists no social welfare system as such, reliance and dependency on one's relatives and friends becomes all the more crucial. In rural Northern Thailand, the *'Wat'* (Thai Buddhist temple) serves as the social centre of the village, where elderly monks can be consulted at times of crisis, whether personal or social, and offer support and counselling, or mediation where necessary to resolve social conflict. Presumably such social intervention or personal support is available to young *kathoey* and their families, should they feel the need for it.

Thailand's 'Ladyboys': an historical note

Kathoey have for centuries formed an integral part of Thai culture (Totman, 2003; Jackson, 2005). As far back as 1636, the Director of the Dutch East India Company, Joult Schouten, noted that in Siam, *'both sexes wear painted petticoats'* (Totman, 2003, p.65). By 1896 males wearing female clothing were observed by Westerners in Chiang Mai (Totman, 2003, p.67) and by the late-nineteenth century a British surveyor had recorded his encounter with an apparently male shop assistant dressed in female attire in Northern Thailand (Totman, 2003, p.69). Moreover, Totman maintains that *kathoey* were performing cabaret dance for public audiences in rural villages in Thailand long before the country became a holiday destination for foreign tourists.

Prior to 1939, 'Siam' was the name of the country that is now known as Thailand. In 1939 the country's then prime minister, Luang Phibunsongkram changed its name from Siam to Thailand. Interactions between different ethnic groups, Mons, Khmer, peoples known as 'Tais', Chinese and Indians for several millennia, have resulted in the construction of 'Thailand' and what is called 'Thai-ness' (Matzner, 2002). Thailand today has one language: 'Thai', and a single national identity. According to Thai creationist myth, the first humans consisted of male, female and hermaphrodite, or *kathoey*. It seems that from the start, *kathoey* were born to 'suffer' because the myth tells of the great love that existed between the first male and the first female, but that this love did not extend to the *kathoey*. In jealousy, according to some sources (for example,

Matzner, 2002; Jackson, 2003), the *kathoey* killed the first woman in order to have the first man to her/himself. Albeit Siamese/Thai cultural myths regarding *kathoey* do differ depending upon whose version one is trying to interpret, we can, nevertheless, safely assume that a 'third gender' has been an integral part of old Siamese and Thai tradition for many centuries. Furthermore, from all readings, whether or not some of these are contradictory, it is noted that the *kathoey* has always held a somewhat ambiguous social status throughout Siamese and Thai history.

However, fires that were caused by Burmese invaders in the late-eighteenth century, destroyed Ayuttaya (then the capital city of Siam), taking with them many historical documents and this is one reason why it is practically impossible to piece together, with any accuracy, a history of Siam and its tradition of transgender prior to that time. Nevertheless, if we look at Totman's account we see that in the sixteenth and seventeenth centuries, Portuguese envoys and European traders observed the Siamese practice of what could these days be described in Western terms as 'cross-dressing'[13] by Siam's men, who wore very similar apparel to that of the country's women. It was also noted that men and women's work roles were undifferentiated in many areas[14] (2003, pp.64-65).

Thus, *kathoey* would perhaps not have been recognised as such by European or other Western visitors to Siam, who would have observed both sexes doing the same work and this, together with the dress similarity, meant they could probably not tell the difference, for, as anthropologist Victor Turner postulates,

> *As members of society, most of us see only what we expect to see, and what we expect to see is what we are conditioned to see when we have learned the definitions and classifications of our culture (1967, p.95).*

---

13 Though as Jackson correctly notes, one can only 'cross-dress' if apparel is gendered, distinct and separated (see Jackson, 2003; no page numbers in original).

14 Indeed, in Thailand today it is not unusual to see women of all ages working alongside men on construction sites.

Hence, *kathoey* would, in all likelihood, have been invisible to the Western eye. However, by the late-nineteenth century, a British Consul and Judge in Siam, W.A.R. Wood, was writing about his observations of, '... *a certain number of men who habitually wear female clothing and grow their hair long...*' (Cited in Totman, 2003, pp.67-68). Wood further observed that there seemed to be nothing remarkable about this phenomenon of *'Pu-mias'* (Trans: 'men-women'). Neither were such people viewed as 'morally wrong' or eccentric by Siamese society (Totman, 2003, p.68).

Jackson (2003) notes that Western visitors to old Siam observed (with notable disdain it seems) the Siamese 'barbarous' culture of scantily dressed people and the practice of polygamy. They reported their own inability to differentiate between Siamese male and female genders. Regardless of gender, hair was cut short, and combed or brushed back away from the face, and difference in male and female fashions did not exist, making gender recognition difficult for the Western 'naïve' observer.

The 'naked' upper bodies of Siamese women as well as men shocked other European visitors to Siam in the late-seventeenth century. While the breasts of young females were covered, older women of childbearing age went naked above the waist (Jackson, 2005). The Siamese tradition of androgyny, where males and females dressed scantily and similarly, with little or no differentiation, began to change following the impact of Western and other foreign visitors' negative reactions that disrupted such traditional gender norms, in favour of more 'civilised' practices (Jackson, 2003; no page numbers in original; Jackson, 2005). This change of dress code was instigated by the Siamese King Mongkut (reigned 1851-1868) in response to the Western-centric criticisms of Siamese culture as 'barbarous' (Jackson, 2003) and the desire for a change to a 'civilised' society borne out of fear of potential Western colonisation of Siam. The hair of women and girls was grown long, all females' upper bodies were covered, and males began to wear trousers rather than the traditional loosely positioned 'loin cloth' type garment of yesteryears. Where once the Western gaze observed 'ugly' women and 'feminine' men (Jackson, 2003; 2005) could now be observed 'beautiful' women and less feminine men. Women's 'beauty' however, began to conform to the Western stereotypical model of feminine beauty. It is noteworthy that today's *kathoey* conform to this precise socially constructed Western stereotype!

Western perceptions of *kathoey*

Since the Second World War, the effects of globalization, Western cinematic and other media influences have meant that with regard to sex, gender and eroticism, Thailand has become, according to Jackson, '... *increasingly integrated into the Western-dominated World order'* (Jackson, 2003; no page numbers in original).[15] Pre-World War Two, there appeared no press reports of 'cross-dressing' in Bangkok or central regions of Siam, but post-World War Two saw a notable rise in press reports on *kathoey* appearing in the Thai media. In contemporary, popular culture in Thailand, *kathoey* are represented in various media productions including films and television soap operas, as well as, indeed, the spectacle of the *kathoey* beauty contest highly prevalent in rural as well as urban regions of Thailand. It is noteworthy that Jackson now regards the 'modern *kathoey*' as having grown up alongside the new 'gay identities' as 'one aspect of the broader gender revolution' that has occurred in Thailand over the past forty years (2003; no page numbers in original). In the past, Western researchers have explained the *kathoey* phenomenon in terms of Western concepts, for example, 'transvestite', 'transgendered male', and 'hermaphrodite'. However, while it is useful to take a cross-cultural analytical look at the different groups that we regard as 'transgender', it seems to me to be problematic to impose one very different culture's interpretation of a phenomenon onto another.

Firstly, let us take a look at the description, 'transvestite'. The term 'transvestite' in Western society refers to (mainly heterosexual) men who, while they feel the need or desire to transitorily adopt the attire of women (as Ekins terms it, 'oscillating' between gender presentations) have no desire to alter, surgically or otherwise, their 'sexed' bodies and 'become' women on a permanent social and legal basis. Western researchers and, indeed tourist business advertisers, frequently refer to 'Transvestite

---

15 It could be argued that, in some respects, Bangkok, Thailand's capital city has become 'Westernized', with its sophisticated, high quality shopping malls, and a public transport system that now includes 'Sky Trains'. Chiang Mai, Phuket and Pattaya are three more cities that have western-influenced shopping malls.

Cabaret shows' in which *kathoey* entertainers perform as dancers. I would contend that the Western term 'transvestite' does not adequately convey or describe the essence of what defines the *kathoey* in Thailand. Calling *kathoey* 'transvestites' misrepresents their own unique sexual/gender identity and totally misses the cultural indigenous meaning attached to the phenomenon. While some *kathoey* may not desire or aspire to undergo sex reassignment surgery, this does not mean they fit the Western concept of 'transvestite'. Moreover, any attempt to categorise them as such suggests a failure to recognise or understand the *kathoey* phenomenon and neglects to embrace an appreciation of the unique sense of self that *kathoey* in this category possess. In my view, *kathoey* are a gender — or genders — in their own right. We cannot assume to construct for them a gender status as indistinguishable from women, for this is to deny them their special and exceptional identities. Some *kathoey* are 'true transsexuals' (in the medical sense) and desire to feminize their bodies with hormones and surgery and to live permanently in the female gender role. For other 'male-femaling' *kathoey*, while their daily presentation of self is that of the female, are content to partially feminize their bodies, but stop short of full sex reassignment surgery. In this category, I found some *kathoey* claiming that they enjoy the 'female' parts of their bodies that exist in juxtaposition with male genitalia, and had no intention of undergoing genital surgery. While others contemplated surgery, this was not a priority and for the present they were content to use hormones to induce breast growth and the prospect of undergoing genital surgery was not an immediate consideration but something that may or may not take place at some future date.

Non-Thais often translate the term *'kathoey'* as 'gay' or 'homosexual'. However, such Westernised concepts of 'gay' or 'homosexual' again fail to capture and hence, inadequately convey the complexities of cultural meaning of *kathoey*. Such simplistic labels serve only to impose Western ideology onto Thai culture, which in turn fails to convey the uniquely intrinsic nature or character of the *kathoey*. We cannot define *kathoey* in terms of Western cultural meaning because it's meaning, even amongst Thais themselves, is ambiguous (ten Brummelhuis, 1999; Totman, 2003; my own fieldwork observations, 2001-02; 2003-04 confirm this view). The term *'kathoey'* serves to describe individuals who fall outside of not only the gender-normative categories of 'male' and 'female' but also those whose sexual orientation is not 'heterosexual'. Most commonly *'kathoey'* refers to transgendered individuals who were born 'male' but adopt the 'opposite' gender role, in varying degrees, in their everyday and working lives. It encompasses, then, those who might fall under the medical definition of 'true transsexuals', as well as all positions along to the opposite end of the gender continuum, and including those whose sexual orientation is homosexual, although Thais, including *kathoey* themselves, differ in their own interpretations of the category. For example, a Thai woman once drew my attention to a person I would describe as an effeminate gay young man, stating, *'He is kathoey!'* On another occasion, whilst I was having lunch in a Bangkok restaurant with a *kathoey*, she herself pointed out, somewhat conspiratorially, and not a little disdainfully, that the young effeminate male waiter who served us was, *'not a true man (mai poo-chai tem tua), he is gay!'* In Thailand, I encountered, then, differing categories of *'kathoey'*. Indeed, *kathoey* themselves differentiate between *'kathoey jing'* (Trans: 'real *kathoey*') who dress and self identify as female and have sex with 'real' (heterosexual-identifying) men and *'kathoey mai jing'* (Trans: 'not real *kathoey*') who dress in male or androgynous attire, may or may not wear subtle makeup, and have sex with gay-identifying men.

Secondly, the term 'transgendered male' inadequately describes *kathoey*. Those whom one could call 'Thai male-to-female transsexuals', in terms of the medical model of the phenomenon, would reject the concept of themselves as 'males' at all. In Thailand, the *kathoey* halts the masculinization process by the ingestion of female hormones at a very young age, not uncommonly before puberty. Thus, the *kathoey* may have been a boy, but has never been a man. Perhaps a more appropriate term might be 'transgendered women' or, 'transsexual women'? However, given that there appear to be different categories of *kathoey*, not all *kathoey* self-identify as transsexual women.

Thirdly, the term 'hermaphrodite' is problematic in that it takes on a Western medical definition that assumes the *kathoey* is intersexed (that is, possessing physical sex characteristics of both male and female) at birth. While there may well be intersexed people amongst the Thai population, (and, indeed, Thai culture would in all probability classify these as 'kathoey') my research did not discover any among the kathoey population of Thailand.[16] The only reason that kathoey in this study have both male and female sex characteristics, is because such bodily formations have been artificially induced either surgically or by ingesting hormones. However, some kathoey view themselves as what could be described as 'hermaphrodite'. Some describe feelings of having a 'female heart' and the 'mind of a woman', that coexist alongside male genitalia and hormone or surgically induced breasts.[17]

The term 'kathoey', then, as we can see, is difficult to define because it's meaning is so ambiguous.[18] As I have explained, the term is variously used to describe disparate groups and typologies of individuals, describing, inter alia, male-to-female transsexuals who have undergone, or aspire to undergo sex reassignment surgery, and who have felt themselves to be female since a very early age. It is worthy of note that this distinctly parallels the experience of the transsexual women in the English sample of this study, who reported, similarly, that they had felt themselves to be 'girls' not 'boys', when they were children. 'Kathoey' also describes those individuals who have feminised their bodies by the use of hormones, breast enlargement surgery or facial feminisation surgery, but who prefer to keep their male genitals, so choose not to undergo sex reassignment surgery. This group I would define as transgender (an umbrella term), but not transsexual (a specific category in the medical definition of the term). Although they keep the male genitals kathoey in this group are invariably of feminine presentation, and their female verisimilitude has led to confusion, even violence in some cases, when 'naïve' Western men mistake these 'virtual' women for 'real' women, only to find themselves, in a sexual encounter, confronted with a penis. Thai women have been known to express envy of the 'beauty' and 'femininity' of kathoey, for example, as one middle-aged Thai woman once said to me, '... they

16 This is not, however, to suggest that intersex people do not exist within the Thai population.

17 It goes without saying that we cannot ignore the subjective experience of those we study.

18 It is worth taking a look at Jackson (1995, p.193) for a discussion on the possible etymological origins of the term 'kathoey'.

[kathoey] are more beautiful than we are'. So central are femininity and beauty to the transgender phenomenon in Thailand that regular *kathoey* beauty contests take place in various venues around the country.

In the Thai language a gender-specific 'polite particle' is used at the end of a sentence, to make it sound more polite. The polite particle is gender-specific according not to the gender of the listener, but to the gender of the speaker. The polite particle used by males is *'krup'* and the polite particle used by females is *'ka'*, and it is this word *'ka'* that is used by all *kathoey* in their everyday speech. Moreover, when speaking English, *kathoey*, and indeed Thais in general, use the female personal pronouns 'she' and 'her',[19] when referring to *kathoey*. However, from my observations, the behaviour of many *kathoey* is sexually brash in a way that the behaviour of Thai women, even those working in the sex industry, is not.

In my view, *kathoey* are not the same as homosexual males and they do not identify with gay men. Neither are they an alternative way of accommodating homosexuality in a more easily facilitated social environment. In Thai society, according to Andrew Matzner, sexual orientation is perceived as being linked with gender identity (Matzner, 2004). For example, that which in the West we call homosexuality (erotic desire for the same sex as oneself) is viewed as cross-gender (transgender) identity in Thailand. For Matzner (2004), transgender (*kathoey*) self identity is perceived as having a 'female mind' and this is different to being 'gay'. Gay men in Thailand are, according to Matzner *'... gender-normative, masculine identified males who are sexually attracted to other gender-normative, masculine-identified males'* (Matzner, 2004, no page numbers in original).[20]

---

19 Personal pronouns are not gender-specific, however, in Thai language.

20 By way of contrast, and to build upon the picture of transgender in Thailand, it is worth briefly considering masculine-identified females in Thailand, and their feminine-identified female partners. Women who are erotically attracted to other women are not perceived as 'lesbians' within the context of Thai culture, but are identified as 'Toms' and 'Dees' (Sinnott, 1999; 2002; 2004). The word 'Tom' is derived from the English language word 'tomboy', and broadly refers to the Thai equivalent of the concept of 'butch' identified 'lesbian' that exists within the Western context. The word 'Dee' derives from the English language word 'lady' (lay-dee) and equates to the 'femme' identified 'lesbian' that exists within the Western context of the concept (Sinnott, 1999, 2004; Jackson, 1999; Matzner, 2004), although it is not useful to interpret other cultural phenomena in terms of Western concepts. Toms and Dees would reject the Western term 'lesbian' as derogatory (Sinnott, 2004).

Kathoey and prostitution

It is a common perception that *'kathoey'* equates to 'transgendered prostitute' and research suggests that *kathoey* are indeed heavily represented in the sex industry, as an alternative career. They are predominantly found in the Bangkok Red Light districts of Patpong and Nana, in Pattaya, further North in Chiang Mai, and in the South in Phuket. For a *kathoey* hailing from an impoverished home in rural Thailand, the sex trade provides a lucrative option and with only a minimum education, her economic status changes from low to high, as she is able to earn enough money to fulfil the cultural imperative and filial duty to support her family, sometimes educating her siblings and buying a home for her parents.

Traditionally, *kathoey* have been used as a sexual outlet for young unmarried Thai men, as a safer option than unmarried young women, in whom virginity is culturally valued and would not want to risk becoming pregnant. Hence, one colloquial term for *kathoey* is *'poo-ying praphet sorng'* or 'a second kind of woman' (Jackson, 1995; 1999; ten Brummelhuis, 1999; Morris, R.C., 1994; Totman, 2003; Costa and Matzner, 2007). *Kathoey* prostitutes then, cater not only to the tourist sex trade, but to Thai males also. However, although *kathoey* seem to be heavily represented in the sex industry, this in no way suggests that they are exclusively employed on the sex scene. Jackson reports that while the *'... kathoey role transcends socio-economic class ... kathoey prostitution appears to be class specific'* (1995, p.189), by which he means, presumably, that *kathoey* prostitutes are from lower socio-economic backgrounds. However, while I would agree with Jackson's view to some extent, in that his statement is generally correct, there are in fact exceptions. Not all of the *kathoey* sex workers I met were from poor rural backgrounds. To examine this further, we need to look more closely at Thai cultural specifics and nuances, and to examine the context within which *kathoey* engage in sex, and the relationship between the *kathoey* and her sexual partner and whether or not she was paid. Some *kathoey* I spoke to referred to their 'boyfriends' when it later became clear that these 'boyfriends' gave them money when sex took place. Furthermore, a *kathoey* would speak of her 'boyfriends' in the plural, describing how one, for example, was American, another was Thai and perhaps yet another was Japanese. In some cases, two or even three of these 'boyfriends' gave her money at the time the sex took place. Is such a relationship, then, a normative boyfriend-girlfriend relationship, or is it prostitution by another name? One such *kathoey*, a university graduate hailing from a middle-class family reported that she regularly got paid for sex with various foreign men she had met while working part-time in a bar when she was an undergraduate student. Other *kathoey* have one 'steady' *farang*[21] 'boyfriend' who visits Thailand two or three times a year and makes regular monetary transfers from his bank to hers while he is away from Thailand. The *kathoey*, in between visits, carries on doing sex work, but devotes her time to her 'steady' boyfriend whenever he is visiting Thailand. It is not uncommon for a 'wealthy' *farang* or other foreign boyfriend to purchase a house for the parents of their *kathoey* girlfriend who hails from a lower class background[22].

Kathoey and Prostitution: understanding the motivation

A considerable contribution to Thailand's economy is provided by prostitution and sex tourism. Indeed, Thailand's tourist sex industry has been viewed as the 'mainstay' of the country's developing economy (Bishop and Robinson, 1998, p.13). It is generally accepted that sex tourism in Thailand began in the 1960s during the Vietnam War[23], when Thailand made an agreement with the US Government to provide 'R and R' (Rest and Recreation) facilities for GIs. American servicemen, employed in active service in Vietnam, would go to Thailand on leave (see, for example, Bishop and Robinson, 1998; UN, 1991:45 cited in Montgomery, 2001, p.40). Young American soldiers, viewed as wealthy in comparison to Thai

---

21 '*Farang*' means 'Western foreigner'.

22 A *kathoey* acquaintance once proudly told me that her *farang* boyfriend had made her parents very happy by buying them a house that cost one million baht (approximately £16,000 in the conversion rate of that time).

23 Before the Vietnam War, in the 1930s, however, Chinese women sex workers were imported from China to serve Chinese immigrants in Thailand (UN, 1991, p.45 in Montgomery, 2001, p.40).

standards of living, soon began to boost the country's economy, paying well for sex and entertainment with young, passive Thai women prostitutes. In order to understand the *kathoey*'s motivation for earning a living through prostitution, we need to examine the issue from the point of view of the *kathoey*, whilst placing it within the context of Thai culture and society as a whole. In Thailand, where few people are privileged to enjoy more than an elementary education, real earning power is severely limited for many. Added to this is the Thai cultural tradition of the 'debt of gratitude' owed by children to their parents for first bringing them into the world, and second, supporting and raising them. This 'debt of gratitude' needs to be repaid as soon as the child reaches an age when he or she is employable in some way. However, as Montgomery (2001) discusses on issues of child prostitution in Thailand, the question is, what exactly defines a child and at what age does a child become an adult? Such conceptual issues are culturally specific, meaning that what constitutes 'the child' in postmodernist Western society is in no way replicated as such a concept in other cultures, and this is certainly the case with Thailand. The young person, then, who hails from a poor family in an impoverished rural village in Thailand, is culturally bound to find employment that pays enough money to not only support themselves, but also to regularly send money home to help support parents, grandparents and younger siblings. Viewed in this light, it becomes clear that while some *kathoey* are, in the neuroscientific sense, 'female in the brain'; others see the *kathoey* life as a means to an end. It seems that some *kathoey* may eventually leave the trans-life and return to their villages, marry and father children. However, I have no evidence to substantiate this notion, aside from odd comments from Thais I encountered during the course of my fieldwork.

In contrast to a 'clownish' stereotype (Totman, 2003) portrayed by Thai popular media, some Western researchers perceive *kathoey* as young, submissive 'feminine' partners for older and more dominant heterosexual men. As discussed above, some assert that all *kathoey* perceive themselves not as males, but as women, or 'a second kind of woman' or a 'Third sex' in a culture where not a bipolar, but a 'tripartite'[24] gender paradigm

---

24 However, as stated elsewhere in this chapter, Buddhist scriptures describe four genders.

exists (Morris, 1994, p.19). Jackson reports that in any sexual transaction, the *kathoey* '... *will almost always be the passive party*' (1995, p.190). In fact I suggest that this is not always the case, contradicting reports of male Western researchers. The data of my research uncover an eclectic group of *kathoey* when it comes to sexual practices. It is not possible to categorize all *kathoey* as the same; they cannot be lumped together under the same umbrella.[25] It is the case that *kathoey* regularly have sex with each other, and a certain number of *kathoey* enhance their earning potential by marketing themselves as '*sao siabp*' [Translation: 'girl who penetrates' or 'penetrating girl'; or 'active Ladyboy']. In Thailand I became aware of *kathoey* prostitutes who specifically market themselves as '*sao siabp*'. Such a self-identity proves to be very lucrative and is particularly appealing to certain male sex tourists who find the experience of being anally penetrated by a 'beautiful girl' appealing enough for them to travel to Thailand and pay well for this sexual service. A 'penetrating girl' is identified as a stereotypically and conventionally 'beautiful' and 'feminine' female, having feminised her body with breast augmentation surgery and/or facial feminization surgery. Like the majority of *kathoey*, they have grown their hair long and wear skilfully applied makeup and long, manicured, painted fingernails.

Another example that falls outside of Jackson's 'passive partner' image of *kathoey* is found in *kathoey* who do not work in the sex industry as such, but in their sexual relations with men will occasionally take the dominant role and anally penetrate their partner. I once observed three *kathoey* friends joking ('*poot len*') about their sexual exploits with men. One claimed that the penis of one man with whom she had engaged in casual sex was so small she told him that her own penis was bigger than his and proceeded to anally penetrate him. The implication being that, even though she was a 'girl', she was a better 'man' than he was.

A further example also refutes Jackson's 'passive partner' image of ~~kathoey~~. In one Bangkok bar I observed on a number of occasions, a

25 For example, the notion that all *kathoey* self-identify as heterosexual women is refuted somewhat by some of my own encounters with *kathoey*; when visiting *kathoey* bars, I was on occasion propositioned by *kathoey* who assumed my presence to mean I was a female sex tourist.

kathoey in a category all of her own. Dressed in black, wearing fishnet stockings held up by suspenders, a tight bodice that emphasised a very narrow waist and breasts and buttocks so large they could surely only have been the result of silicone implants. Her face was heavily made up with highly arched eyebrows, eye shadow and sparkling 'diamonds' decorating her eyelids; white pencil lines defined and elongated her nose. I never learnt her name, but her startling appearance and menacing demeanour led me to name her, euphemistically (but not unkindly), 'The Dominatrix'. My British male companion, who had nobly accompanied me on fieldwork visits to *kathoey* bars, readily confessed to having found her 'rather frightening', and although I refer to her here in the female pronoun, I could not in truth classify her as female or feminine, and pondered on her subjective self-identity and sexuality, which, one could argue, are the most important. However, I admit to being confounded as to how I could classify her.

Notwithstanding the fact that this *kathoey* (i.e. the 'Dominatrix') and others working in the same bar use the female gender polite particle, 'ka' in their everyday speech, from my observations in this bar, and from a female perspective, I would again challenge the generally perceived notion that all *kathoey* self-identify exclusively as female. While some of these individuals were simply not feminine, they were, however, (with the exception of 'The Dominatrix') to my eyes at least, *effeminate*. It was not only their appearance, but also their behaviour that separated them from the female sex, for watching them dancing on the stage, my interpretation of what I observed was a group of *boys*, who were not very good at dancing, 'doing female', or 'male-femaling' and were neither masculine nor feminine, homosexual nor heterosexual, but a confusing aggregate of all of these. Their 'transitional journey' then, only took them as far as they needed to go to suit their employment prospects, rather than, as in the case of 'true transsexuals', to full sex reassignment surgery. It is as though they are 'playing' with gender in such a way as to enhance their careers as sex workers. Indeed on another occasion when I had visited a Bangkok bar with a group of friends, a *kathoey* who had joined us to our astonishment proceeded to squeeze her right nipple, out of which squirted a liquid that could only have been breast milk.

Curious as to how this biological impossibility could have occurred, we asked a *kathoey* friend, who had accompanied us to the bar, for an explanation. She informed us that some *kathoey* bar workers take large overdoses of hormone injections, as well as hormone tablets and that this had the desired effect. The *kathoey* who had performed the 'party piece' for us had male genitals; in such cases, *kathoey* are quite literally, 'betwixt and between' genders.[26]

Kathoey and non-sex industry employment

As mentioned earlier, *kathoey* are represented in all walks of social life and in both urban and rural locations. *Kathoey* work as teachers (of children as well as adults in the commercial world); as retail assistants[27]; hospital receptionists; guesthouse proprietors; tour guides; tour operators; hairdressers; beauty therapists and (theatrical) makeup artists. Indeed, I once observed a *kathoey* immigration officer, resplendent in the female uniform, working at Bangkok airport. Perhaps the most 'glamorous' of *kathoey* careers, however, is that of the professional cabaret dancer.

In tourist districts of Thailand, cabaret shows feature not only transgendered performers, but *kathoey* beauty contests, where the audience is subjected to the spectacle of dozens of *kathoey* beauty contestants, parading the catwalks resembling the male-constructed stereotypical 'Barbie Doll' image of what could be termed, 'feminine beauty'. In the main, *kathoey* work hard at accomplishing a feminine presentation. Traditionally it is quite common for an older *kathoey* to act as mentor or 'sister' to an aspiring *kathoey*, tutoring and admonishing their pupil in all aspects of the *kathoey* life (Totman, 2003). *Kathoey* dancers train assiduously to perfect their choreographic skills and feminine presentation, and only the best are offered the opportunity to work in the high-quality, more sophisticated cabaret shows in major cities and towns

---

26 This was an observable example of the 'performativity' of gender, albeit a rather astonishing, even shocking construction of gender.

27 I once observed a *kathoey* working in a Tesco supermarket, in Phuket. She wore a combination of the uniforms worn by women and men: the trousers worn by male employees and the dress worn by female employees. I pondered on the likelihood of such a scenario in Tesco's in the UK!

in Thailand, such as Alcazar and Tiffany's in Pattaya, Simon Cabaret in Phuket, Calypso in Bangkok and Simon Cabaret in Chiang Mai.

So *kathoey* celebrate their gender! But while both transsexual women in England and *kathoey* in Thailand both suffer social stigma, for the *kathoey* such suffering is associated with bad karma, whereas the British transwomen of this study reported their suffering as emotional due to lack of social acceptance and rejection by family, as well as discrimination in other areas such as the workplace. However, the difference is the fact that *kathoey* on the face of it tend to 'celebrate' and enjoy their lives as virtual women.[28] On a daily basis one can observe *kathoey* on the streets of Thailand, coquettishly flaunting[29] their 'feminine' presentation, their feminine characteristics (almost satirically) exaggerated, a veritable pastiche of a woman. Spending time with different *kathoey* on a one-to-one basis and doing 'normal' everyday activities, such as visiting a beauty parlour for a facial or a manicure, meant the opportunity arose for me to observe the Goffmanesque 'presentation of self in everyday life' of *kathoey*. Their 'male-femaling' situation-specific, as some *kathoey* will take on the role of 'court jester', or 'comedy entertainer', as they flirt with taxi drivers, shop or restaurant proprietors, or beauty therapists, joking and laughing. *Kathoey* also have a reputation in the derogatory sense; and this is likely due in part to their portrayal by the Thai media as, 'loud-mouthed', 'exhibitionist' and 'uncouth' (Totman, 2003, p.62).

Here, I have attempted to capture for you the transgender phenomenon in Thailand. The study of transgender subjectivities captures for us how the inner social world works, and indicates how the interior world of the transsexual person is radically affected by the social world, which they inhabit. Studying the subjectivities of transgender folk requires more than theory. It requires fieldwork and ethnography, in order to build and expand on the theories and philosophies of theorists and other critical thinkers. My study of virtual women then, is grounded in

---

28 However, I did in fact meet *kathoey* who fell outside of this group. See for example, the stories of Emma and Pui.

29 In contrast, transwomen in England tend to strive for 'stealth', in an endeavour to blend in rather than flaunt their transgender status.

ethnography and qualitative interviews and is, therefore, informed by the personal narratives of the transsexual women and *kathoey* themselves. In the following chapters, I let these virtual women speak for themselves ...

CHAPTER FOUR

On Becoming a Woman
Dressing up and Coming Out

Introduction

Let us now explore the various stages — or rites of passage — that the British virtual women of my study experienced on the road to transition, as compared to the more easily facilitated transition of *kathoey* in Thailand. Recall that in this book I attempt to interpret the transgender experience from the point of view of the transgendered individual. Thus, throughout the chapter I intersperse the narratives of British transwomen and *kathoey* so that their voices are heard. Characteristically, many of the British transsexual women in this study reported having felt 'different' from a very early age, and by some chance discovered that the incongruence they experienced between their gender identity and physical body was due to transsexualism. The popular description of the male-to-female transsexual is 'a woman trapped inside a man's body'. However, I suggest that such a phrase is a simplistic one, and fails to consider the complexities that transsexualism embraces. The discovery of transsexualism can be often so traumatic or distressing that the individual will either decide to try and ignore the problem, or suffer in silence in the hope that it will 'go away'. This means that the transsexual individual in England is commonly physically fully matured long before they seek help. The experience of the Thai *kathoey*, however, as will be discussed later in this chapter, sits in striking contrast to that of the British transwoman.

On the Outside Looking In

A common experience as told in the narratives of the British transsexual women in this book is an overwhelmingly marginalizing feeling of 'not fitting in' to mainstream society. Endeavours to 'try and fit in' where there was no legitimate place for them, and the resultant suicidal thoughts and feelings of despair that inevitably accompany such thwarted efforts, form common themes emerging from the data of this study. As Marion, a transsexual woman in her forties told me on the eve of her departure for surgery in Thailand,

... Looking back on it, I have realised that I was very much on the edge of the peer group, you know, I didn't really understand what made these people tick and I wanted to be part of the group. That's what we do isn't it? We want to belong. And there were all these kinds of attitudes and ways of being that were different, and if you'd asked me to, I couldn't put my finger on what they were, I just didn't feel part of it.

Feelings of 'confusion', 'separateness' and of 'not fitting in' the male role dog the British transsexual individuals of this study and lead to deep emotional and psychological distress, that in later life often translates into suicidal contemplations and, as one informant described it, 'complete and utter despair'.[30] Desperate to fit in, subjects variously reported 'striving for acceptance'; working hard to 'emulate guys' in an attempt to 'blend into the male gender', immersing themselves in stereotypically 'male' activities in order to achieve this. On this theme, this is what Tanya had to say:

I knew that I could not act like the guys, so I had to do something, which would give me some kind of respect ...

To this end, Tanya's strategic plan involved taking up motorcycle racing. She continued:

I was so desperate to fit in, in any way I could ... I was just so scared of people finding out, but I didn't know what to do ... I just felt so trapped inside, and I was scared to come out ... scared of the consequences.

Tanya's narrative succinctly expresses and encapsulates what it means to be transsexual and trying to fit in whilst living on the gendered parameters that prevail in British society:

---

30 However, discussions of suicide in relation to trans people need to be treated with caution. This is not to diminish the difficulties experienced by trans people, but the occurrence of suicide attempts amongst this group needs to be analyzed after thorough and judicious examination.

> *... I have never felt for a moment that I was a male. I used
> to try and watch and study men and try and act in the
> way that they did but it was so unnatural. I just couldn't
> do it. For me it was as though I had missed a day at school
> or something and thinking, is there some lesson I had just
> not learned here? I just couldn't do it.*

Nicole described the emotions she experienced as a young 'man' trying
to come to terms with 'his' gender dysphoria: *'I was very unhappy inside
... and I was getting more and more depressed ...';* indeed, others recounted
feelings of unworthiness, of life having no value. For example, in response
to my comment to Tanya that putting herself in a situation with huge
potential for danger, as she did in motorcycle racing, must have required
a great deal of courage, she replied:

> *I think it was just despair at the time. Almost like giving
> up, almost having a death wish — some of the antics you
> get up to on the track ...*

Likewise, Gina stated:

> *'I went into a huge depression ... I didn't care if I was alive
> or dead. I couldn't give a damn ...',*

Other respondents similarly reported feeling that life held no value;
for example, Nicole stated:

> *I couldn't make my life make sense; it didn't mean anything
> ... it had no value attached to it ...*

While Nicole had struggled to make sense of her life, Tanya had become
aware that the root of her problem was her gender dysphoria and that
she needed to transition. However, she was held back from taking that
step by an overwhelming sense that she was not 'strong enough' to go
through with it. She voiced her deep fear of being 'ridiculed, cast out
and kicked out of home', thus:

I was so afraid of … just ending up completely lonely; I mean you read all these stories in the newspapers, all these sensationalist headlines about transsexuals. It is degrading how they put people like us down. I was so scared of people finding out but I didn't know what to do …

And this, in line with what other respondents reported, caused feelings of their (female) gendered selves being imprisoned, locked inside their own heads. As Tanya articulated:

I just felt so trapped inside, and I could not tell anybody and … I was finding it really, really hard to cope …

For Tanya, such a verbalization of the feelings she experienced of her female 'self' being trapped inside a metaphorical prison served to sum up her fears of unlocking the essential internal conflict that other respondents referred to as 'the genie in a box'. Nicole experienced such 'imprisonment' as 'complete and utter despair'; and conveyed the difficulty of adequately expressing one's own feelings so that others can sufficiently understand or empathise. The following excerpt from her interview illustrates this. Asked whether she had ever felt that she fitted the popular description of the transsexual as 'a woman trapped inside a man's body', Nicole had responded that she did not feel like that because, she explained, '*I don't know what it is like to be a woman, I don't know what it is like to be a man, I only know what it is like to be me*'.

She explained it thus:

I've always felt like there has been a separation between me and other people. Like there was always something different. And I used to think that I was — I rationalised it that I had some sort of freak gene that made me somehow different and I couldn't get it any more clearer than that. Or some kind of mistake or something not quite right, that I didn't know what it was.

Kate's early feelings of 'separateness' of being 'apart' and 'different' also echo those felt by Nicole; here is Kate's response:

> I was always conscious that there was something different about me; I just felt I didn't — people didn't sort of — I felt somehow apart from other children and felt different and without really being able to put my finger on what it was ...

However, when Kate changed schools at the age of ten, the explanation as to why she felt 'different' became clear to her:

> ... I changed to an all boys' school and suddenly thought, 'this is all wrong, I shouldn't be here at this school '... it was a boarding school... I was not happy. It felt all wrong. I mean, I'd worked it out what was wrong ... that actually I should have been at a girls' school ...

Another informant described how, as a small boy, 'he' wanted to know why 'he' could not be a girl, adding,

> I remember as a child, feeling like — wanting to know why I couldn't be a girl ... certainly by the time I went to school I had real feelings about being jealous of the girls ...

Feeling 'jealous' or envious of girls was a theme that ran through many of the interviews that I carried out with British transsexual women. Another informant told me she felt that her male body was 'inappropriate' and that she knew 'instinctively' that she was not a boy; that she 'didn't feel like a boy'. Yet another informant simply stated it: 'I have always felt deformed more than anything ...' and this she claimed, was because her head was fine, but her body was wrong. She went on to describe how, as a child, she cried herself to sleep at night, having '... prayed to a god that didn't exist to put me right, oh! put me right'. And this was a common plight: several informants similarly recalled '...praying to god to make me wake up a girl'. Tanya asserted that she had '... never actually *been able to act in the male guise ... my physicality resembled a male, but everything else was female'.*

Sociologist, Irving Goffman (1963) theorizes that each social actor has two selves: the Actual Self and the Virtual Self. Putting my own interpretative slant on this theory, it is this two-sided coin that is a constant source of psychological conflict experienced by the transsexual person in British society. While the male physicality represents the presentation in everyday life of the Virtual Self, the Actual Self is the female within, desperate to emerge and find social acceptance as a legitimate member of society. The irony is, however, that, as I have stated elsewhere in this volume, the fully transitioned transsexual woman can only approximate a change of sex — she remains a 'Virtual Woman'. Susie described the psychological conflict she experienced as a child:

> *... it felt as if there was a battle going on between two people, the person I wanted to be and there was another thing in there, the male side. I always felt that it was not what I want, what I am or what I should be. When I looked in the mirror I didn't see me, a man, I saw me, Susie, always.*

For Marion, however, her childhood conflict was not veiled in confusion; rather her gendered subjectivity, she was adamant, was crystal clear. Discussing the question, 'how does it feel to be a woman?' here is what she had to say:

> *I am quite clear that <u>I am</u>, have <u>always</u> been, <u>and always</u>*
> *<u>wanted to be</u> a woman and <u>should have been a woman</u> and*
> *as some would say, it was by some strange twist of fate that*
> *I wasn't. [Underlining indicates emphasis in tone of voice].*
> AB: *So you feel — ? Well, if you asked me, 'what does it feel like to*
> *be a woman?' I wouldn't be able to tell you — it is something*
> *that is in you, you just know. I was a little girl and now I*
> *am a woman, and it is very difficult to articulate isn't it?*
> M: *Oh, sure, sure —*

AB: *— and it is probably an unfair question, isn't it: 'how does it feel'?*

M: *[Pondering the question] How does it feel? Well, now it is OK, I mean I have come to a huge level of self-acceptance and I have never felt better about myself than I do now ... but, you know, it is just great to <u>be</u> and if you wanted me to speculate on the difference between men and women, I think women are good <u>at being</u>, but men <u>do stuff</u>. Can you see what I mean? [Underlining indicates emphasis in tone of voice]*

AB: *Yes, yes.*

However, notwithstanding Marion's clear understanding and conviction that she 'should have been a girl', like other subjects of this study, she set about hiding her female (actual) Self by immersing herself in stereotypically masculine activities, such as yacht racing, rock climbing, joining the armed forces or undertaking other conventionally 'male' activities, in a bid to 'keep the genie in the box'. One respondent stated: '... *I have been like a chameleon, all my life, constantly changing, trying to find who I am I suppose ...'* And as noted above, Marion speculated that 'the difference between men and women is that women are good at *being*, but men *do stuff* ... reporting: '*and I did a lot of stuff — I was superman!'* Somewhat paradoxically, however, Marion recalled, as a little boy, '... *seeing girls and wanting to wear dresses, and wanting to be my mother's little girl'*.

I would like to now share with you, the reader, some of the experiences of British transsexual women and Thai *kathoey* who recall, as children, dressing in feminine clothes.

Cross-dressing — why the guilty secret?

First of all, let us be clear that the cross-dressing practices of transgendered individuals in England and Thailand differ in one crucial aspect: that of secrecy. The transsexual women in the British sample of this study reported having, since early childhood, experienced the strong desire to dress in the attire of the 'opposite' sex, typically as young as four or five years of age. Such dressing was always done in secret. In contrast, the Thai *kathoey* to whom I spoke recalled female family members (sisters, mothers, aunts) dressing them in their sisters' clothes, yet this was a source of mild amusement, rather than, as in the case of the British subject, a source of embarrassment or humiliation. In stark contrast, *kathoey* on the streets of Thailand invariably openly, indeed coquettishly, flaunt themselves in female attire. Several *kathoey* to whom I spoke recalled, as a small child, being dressed in feminine clothes for various reasons. One *kathoey*, whom I shall call Som, was the first grandchild born to the family. At the age of five she had thought she was herself a girl, and reported the family had 'many girls' indicating that there was perhaps a shortage of boys' clothes available, or that they dressed 'him' as a girl 'for fun'. Som explained[31]:

> ... *my family have many, many girls and lady in family house. And like to put skirt, little skirt on me and like to say "oh, so cute", but they don't think about when I grow up in my mind if lady or a man ... but when I go to school I must to wearing a boy uniform.*
>
> AB: *... so, how did it make you feel when you had to wear boys' clothes to go to school?*
>
> Som: *Nothing in my mind, because I was a child ... I think, as children have no feeling. Nothing in my heart, but then when I grow up and be adult and be teenage, I think, 'Oh! I like ladies' clothes!'*
>
> AB: *So how did it make you feel when you realised in your heart that you wanted to be a girl, but you had a boy's body?*
>
> Som: *Nothing ... no problem ... [although] I have to cut my hair and look like boy, but my action not boy.*
>
> AB: *And when you were at university, did you wear girls' clothes then?*
>
> Som: *Oh yes, because have freedom. I can [wear] makeup; I can have long hair, yes.*

---

31   Some parts of the interview with Som were carried out in English. Som's words are a direct transcription from the interview recording.

In Thai culture, a 'son' is highly valued by both the family and by Thai society at large. As Som reported:

Everybody in Thailand like to have a son. When the baby birth [is born] they say, 'Oh! He is son, he is son!!' and everybody happy.

However, when her family realised Som's *kathoey* status, they were initially less than happy, although they did little to discourage her from adopting the *kathoey* role. Asking Som, 'When you wear feminine clothes, how does it make you feel?' [*Mua khun dtang dto-a bpen poo-ying roo-sOOg yang rai ka?*], brought the response: '*Oh, I feel good, and it gives me confidence*'. However, wearing men's clothes had the opposite effect; Som reported that this made her feel unconfident. These sentiments were echoed by other *kathoey*, one of whom also reported that, like Som, she felt 'very comfortable' in feminine clothes. However, she recalled one occasion when she had to wear male attire for a job interview and this had been for her a source of 'embarrassment' and 'shame', to the point that she hid herself in a taxi because she did not want anybody to see her dressed as a male. It is interesting to speculate that should we reverse such a scenario, by replacing the situation of this *kathoey* in Thailand with that of the transsexual (or 'cross-dresser'), in England by swapping the attire to that of the female, whether it would be likely to produce the same effect on the individual concerned. As one British informant disclosed to me: '*... dressing as a male used to make me feel physically sick. It was horrible*'. Moreover, as noted elsewhere in this book, a 'male' in British society dressed in 'female' attire is likely to attract negative attention with the accompanying ridicule, humiliation and verbal abuse. However, we need to beware of making two simplistic generalizations when comparing transgender in the two countries studied here.

Lek is a fully transitioned post-op *kathoey* who has felt herself to be 'a lady' since she was a small child, and dressed 'like a lady' throughout her childhood. However, she reported the conflict she experienced with her primary school teacher thus:

> *... every time I go to school I want long hair and teacher*
> *want to cut. Cannot take [have] the long hair. And every*
> *time I go home and tell Mama and sometime I cry. And*
> *Mama say, 'OK, you want cut? OK, make like boy'. And I*
> *want hair long like little bit but why cannot be like that?*
> *And next day I take out everything hair –*

AB: *You cut off all of your hair? Cut it all off?*

Lek: *Yes*

AB: *Like a monk?*

Lek: *Yes*

AB: *Because you were angry that they would not let you have*
       long hair, you shaved it all off?

Lek: *Yes*

AB: *Oh. What did they say?*

Lek: *Teacher don't fight me again ... she know I angry with her.*

As a little 'boy' in primary school, Lek was required to wear male attire and behave in the male role. At home, however, while she experienced some antipathy to her transgender status from her father, she nonetheless was free to wear female attire when she was not at school, a situation that falls outside the boundaries of British social limits and would be banned or ridiculed in England.[32]

Although Lek experienced some opposition to her female presentation from her father and teacher, not all *kathoey* in this study reported similar responses. Tinar recalled as a young child being dressed by her sister in female attire, and indeed her family members, in particular her father, had expressed not only no antagonism to her dressing and behaving like

---

32 However, when it came to Western transsexual woman's dress, Lek displayed a judgemental attitude, that resembled more Western social attitudes to transgender than those of Thai culture. Asking Lek the question: 'How does it make you feel when you wear ladies' clothes?' Lek gave this response: 'When I look like a lady, no problem, because I have small body and when somebody looking, no problem, because OK, I have good body, OK... but I tell you one thing; when some farang lady transsexual, ladyman, when [they have a] big body and too big muscles, you know, and when they wear clothes like the lady, this no good.

a girl, but actually wholeheartedly accepting her as *kathoey*.[33] Tinar reported having since the age of five played with girls and with "girls' things"; helping her sister to carry out household chores, while her parents worked in the fields. Tinar remembered enjoying this rather than playing 'rough games with boys'. Here is what she had to say:

> *My sister had to take care of me. I follow my sister because I closer with my sister more than my brothers ... my family is not rich, is medium poor. My other sister is working; my brother is young. So [this] is something I can do for my family, like washing the dishes, everything I have to do like this. I don't mind, I like, because I like clean, and don't like dirty.*

So, albeit Tinar had household responsibilities as a very young child, she was happy in that role and preferred carrying out chores to playing rough games with boys. It is a very different picture for the transsexual 'cross-dressing' in England.

In England: "... no matter what outer appearances were, inside I did not feel like a man ..."

As aforementioned, the fundamental difference between the 'cross-dressers' in England and in Thailand is that while in Thailand this is overt, Western societal and cultural mores serve, by and large, to restrict 'cross-dressing' to covert activity. Hence, somewhat unsurprisingly, all of the transsexual women in this research reported having 'cross-dressed' in secret from a very young age, and this activity was always accompanied by risk-taking and feelings of guilt and fear should the big secret be uncovered. In Thailand, on the other hand, at least for the post-pubertal *kathoey*, dressing in female attire is a fun activity, to be openly enjoyed in public without the disapproval of society in general. British respondents invariably reported having 'borrowed' their mother's or their sister's

---

33 Tinar has two brothers and two sisters, and told me that her father used to joke [Trans: '*poot len*' in Thai language] that he had two and a half sons and two and a half daughters!

clothes, or of having acquired armfuls of clothes at jumble sales and hiding them in their bedrooms, so that they were available for their use, in secret, as soon as the opportunity arose. One informant, Lucy, in her late thirties reported having, as a teenager, identified very strongly with the New Romantics pop music culture genre of the time. One such example is Boy George, a singer who ordinarily wore feminine attire and full feminine-style makeup, off stage as well as on stage. Lucy's identity with this culture served to facilitate her own 'dressing' in the same way as she found an outlet for expression of what she called her 'feminine side'. Another similarly aged informant described dressing as a teenager in *'leggings, high boots and brightly painted, bright red leather jacket, with long hair and heavy Gothic makeup'.* A characteristic of cross-dressing by the British respondents of this study is the fact that some, but by no means all, reported that cross-dressing during and after puberty also involved sexual arousal and autoeroticism, and coupled with this, feelings of self-disgust and self-hatred. The majority of informants reported attempts to 'control it', while another predominantly constant theme exposed in these data was the 'calming effect' that 'dressing' had on the person engaged in the activity. This 'calming effect' was typically preceded by intense anxiety and stressful periods that had built up over time until the point was reached when the person felt the only course of action to relieve such stress was to 'dress'. An insightful example of this is the narrative of Jane, who as a young married man had taken 'his' pregnant wife to the maternity hospital when the birth of their first child was imminent. Jane's wife was fully aware of her husband's cross-dressing and this was an activity that they had done together. Jane described her need to 'dress' as a 'compulsion' that she 'couldn't help' doing and after which *'... for brief periods, I felt better'*; let us now consider some more of Jane's narrative:

Jane: *There was a sort of feeling of, you know, calm; calm and relaxed ...
and it needs to be put into context, of how it was leading up to that.
There were periods when I was very strung up, very on edge, and
things felt bad and unmanageable and then they would feel better.*

However, in common with the reports of other informants in this study, 'feeling better' for Jane was a temporary situation. Reports of deluding themselves, that they were 'able to control' the cross-dressing, weaves through all of the data of the British sample of this research. Jane confessed that, although she had thought she had got her 'dressing' under control, it became evident at the time of the birth of the couple's first child, that this was not the case. We take up Jane's narrative again here :

> ... I took her into hospital for the birth of our first child and there was an absolute dragon of a sister on the [labour] ward of this hospital and she wouldn't let me stay with her. And I didn't have the gumption or the confidence or whatever to say, 'I am jolly well going to stay', and my wife didn't either. I was despatched, sent away. So I went home and was feeling pretty miserable and I dressed up in my wife's clothes ... and I absolutely remember that <u>I simply had to dress up and be in women's clothes.</u> [Underlining indicates emphasis in tone of voice].

AB: *I think that's very interesting.*

Jane: *Yes, mm, yes ...*

Significantly, Jane's 'dressing' was not only normally facilitated by her wife, but she had her own wardrobe of feminine clothes, so the compulsion to dress in her wife's clothes on that occasion is worthy of note. I put it to Jane:

AB: *It is very interesting that in fact you were dismissed from the female domain of childbirth and you felt that the only way that you could get back into it was to go and put on your wife's clothes.*

Jane: *Yes, mm, yes... it was something that I <u>had to do</u>, I <u>absolutely had</u> to do it, I had to identify as closely as possible with what was going on. [Underlining indicates emphasis in tone of voice].*

Jane confessed that she had never told her wife about the incident and indeed, that she had never told anyone else before. The reason she had not told her wife about it, was because, she stated, '... *I felt somehow that I was being disloyal ...*'. Secrecy, then, is a theme that forms an essential element in cross-dressing activity for the pre-transitioned transsexual woman in England and therefore by necessity, this entails, somewhat predictably, a considerable amount of risk-taking.

Risking it!

For Kate, a former high-ranking officer in the Royal Air Force, the risky business of living with dual identities and the dread of discovery were considerable. Living in one town, but working in another, meant not only that she had opportunities to cross-dress, but that the risk factor increased. We take up her narrative here:

Kate: *I took enormous risks! I used to drive up to [town where she worked] on a Sunday night, dressed, and arrive at the house [where she lived during the week] as 'Kate' and emerge the following morning as 'Group Captain Dogsbody!' [laughs].*

Although in October 1967, homosexuality was de-criminalised in England, in the Royal Air Force homosexual activity continued to be viewed as gravely serious misconduct that carried with it court martial proceedings, followed by imprisonment and dishonourable discharge, something of which Kate was only too keenly aware.

> *... so I took <u>enormous</u> risks! I mean, if the RAF had found out what I was doing!!... sooner or later I was going to be caught and, as you yourself pointed out, the armed forces' view on any sort of sexual deviation — transvestism, sado-masochism, all those things were to be classed as 'homosexual' and were treated as very serious cases ...*

Kate's concern about the acute distress and embarrassment that 'getting caught' would inevitably bring upon her wife and children, as well as other family members, prompted her to leave the RAF and find employment in a less restricting environment, in the hope that, should her cross-dressing become known, the consequences would be less serious than had it happened whilst she was serving in the armed forces.

Despite Kate's light-hearted recollections of her pre-transitional life, we cannot lose sight of the fact that the transsexual person's life is typically fraught with difficulty, emotional distress, and depression and, in the words of several of the transsexuals in this study, 'despair'.

Despair

I got more and more depressed,
more and more unhappy,
and less and less able to cope ...
(Nicole, interview, 2002)

All of the British transsexual women I spoke to told me that, despite their attempts to 'fit in' as male social actors within a socially bipolar gender system, their efforts proved fruitless, and perhaps inevitably, this led to feelings of depression, in all cases thoughts of suicide and in some cases, attempted suicide. Nicole recalled the time at which her gender dysphoria reached such intensity that she was facing suicide:

> *I started crying my eyes out, crawling around on the floor, complete and utter despair, didn't know what the hell was going on ...*

And when her mental and emotional distress reached overwhelming proportions:

> *... I decided, you know ... I really had nothing to lose. Because at that point, I was just about facing suicide; I thought this is so shit; life is so shit... just pain and unhappiness, rejection and ugliness. So I thought, you know, I'll give it one last chance and if it doesn't work out, just go and top myself.*

And others echoed Nicole's sentiments:

'I hate to admit it, but I actually contemplated suicide';

'It all began to become so obvious and clear and started on a vicious depressive spiral downwards'; '... I was beginning to feel suicidal — I couldn't cope... I thought, what's the point in living?';

'I became desperately depressed ... it became very difficult to actually cope to the extent that I came close to a nervous breakdown'.

Whereas one informant reported coming close to a nervous breakdown, another informant, Samantha, reported that having considered suicide 'on two or three occasions' at the age of fifteen; at twenty-one she had a nervous breakdown. Another informant, Angela, recounted:

I was in such turmoil; I didn't know what to do. I was in a lot of distress ... I had got to the point where I was suicidal ... a crashing depression... and I knew that I either had to face a life of depression and potential suicide, or transition ... I realized I had no choice but to transition ...

Discovering the Trans-Self: "Finding Out" – England:

A common theme that runs through the British sample of this study is the way that the transsexual person first discovered that the confused feelings they experienced around their gender identity were articulated in the autobiographies of other transsexual women. Another source of explanation came in the form of sensationalist tabloid newspaper reports. Nicole recalled being in her late teens when the realization had dawned on her that her intense distress and confusion might be due to transsexualism, after discovering the story in a tabloid newspaper of a high-profile male-to-female transsexual:

Caroline Cossey was in the Sunday papers, and I remember seeing that, and ... there she was, this absolutely fantastic beautiful woman who was this transsexual. I walked home reading it and read it again, read it again, read it again and then I panicked! I thought, "Jesus Christ, is that me? Is this what's happening to me?" You know, I mean, this was the most coherent explanation of what was happening to me that I had seen until I read that paper. I was 19. I remember keeping that article and pictures and I hid it... I was petrified that anyone else would see. I didn't want anybody else knowing I was interested in that... so that sort of got buried.[34]

Others reported having read, at a very young age, the stories of British transsexual "April Ashley" or American tennis player "Renee Richards" in the *News of the World* or other tabloids, while others recalled reading articles on transsexuals in their mother's "women's magazines". As adults, others had read the autobiographies of transsexual women, for example, Jan Morris' *Conundrum*, (1997/1974), or Renee Richards' *Second Serve: Renee Richards Story* (1983). Here is what Kate had to say:

> *... I went into a bookshop and I found Conundrum — it had just come out. And in, that [book] there was somebody to whom I could relate.*
>
> AB: *And was that the first time you realised that it was possible to change gender?*
>
> Kate: *Yes, the first time that I knew that it was possible for someone like me — I mean, I may have known subliminally that something could be done, but I didn't think people like me did that sort of thing and Jan Morris's book was a big revelation. I bought the book with trembling hands and ... I got home and I read the book and I couldn't believe*

---

34 The terms 'buried', 'banked' or 'hacking it back down' were used variously by the British subjects of this research to describe the way they tried to deny the reality of their gender dysphoria.

*that this was somebody like me ... somebody who had got
the same sort of background that I had had ... I'd been in
the RAF, she had been in the Army and had led a sort of
successful masculine life and by this time I'd had children
and a successful RAF career.*

AB: *So, did it make everything worse for you then?*

Kate: *In some ways, it did. There was something that could be done,
but I couldn't do anything. So it made things worse from
that point of view... I just read that book, over and over and
my wife and I had debates on whether I was transsexual or
not and I mean a lot of self-delusion went on — I mean, I
would say, 'oh, no, I can't be, here I am, I am married to you,
I have got this job, and I can't do it'. I mean, the last thing
my wife wanted to hear was me saying I was transsexual.*

Gina, a transsexual woman in her forties, recalled realizing at the age
of twelve, that she was transsexual, having read the April Ashley story
in the *News of the World*:

> *... maybe I didn't have it [the knowledge that she was
> transsexual] as a distinct conscious feeling, but yeah, I guess
> that was pretty much behind what I felt. But then I found
> out what I was when I was twelve years old ... the April
> Ashley thing hit the papers ... and I can remember taking the
> papers into the bathroom or toilet to read them in secret ...*

The salient point here is Gina's need to read the Ashley story *in secret*;
this reluctance to talk about the gender confusion they experienced was
a common theme running through the data from the British sample of
this study. Not all were fortunate to have a supportive partner. At twelve,
Gina's enlightenment about her transsexual status, like that of Kate served
no good purpose in finding the help she needed, as she explains:

> *... and I read it and was fascinated and I knew that was
> exactly what I am — it offered an answer in one way; I*

thought, yes, it is possible, you can grow up to be a woman, but at the same time it is impossible, because who the hell could I tell at twelve years old? No one would believe me — they would just think I was completely weird! They'd lock me up! ... I would be derided, castigated, whatever, and just be considered completely abnormal and strange. So I didn't say anything to anyone.

Marion also expressed her fears of the consequences of revealing to anyone her gender confusion; she claimed that at the age of eight she had read the story in a women's magazine about an American surgeon who had 'created beautiful [transsexual] women', and realised that perhaps she too was one such person, and that there was perhaps some remedy for her gender confusion:

... and I thought, 'God! This is possible!' I remember very clearly it said that it was one in a million and that young boys often grew up confused about what came to be called 'gender identity'... but they grew out of it. And it was like, 'Oh, OK, right, well it is going to go away, I don't need to tell anybody about this'... and, it would go away, so I kept it buried and lived with it, day in, day out, cross-dressing of course.

As we shall now discover, however, the case of the Thai *kathoey* is very different. For the *kathoey*, secrecy in cross-dressing does not come into the equation. The transgender landscape in Thailand contrasts distinctly from that in England.

Discovering the *kathoey* Self — Thailand

The young *kathoey* growing up in Thailand escapes much of the trauma that the British transsexual person suffers on discovering their transgender status, and this is likely to be due to Thailand's culturally ubiquitous *kathoey* population. Typically, asking *kathoey* how they came about learning that it is possible to change gender, brought the almost universal response that they had another family member who was *kathoey*, or a childhood friend who lived in the same street, or a school friend who was *kathoey* themselves and so recognised it in others. Finding out they were *kathoey* was not an earth-shattering event; rather it was something that was observable and obvious to all around them, by their gendered behavioural traits. As one *kathoey* simply put it: *'people realise when they are like me ...'* A *kathoey* I interviewed in Bangkok stated: *'In my heart, I am a woman; inside, I feel like a woman ...'* and that she had felt like that since the age of 'four or five'. Gop, a *kathoey* I met in Northern Thailand told me that she had always felt like a girl, since the age of about four years, and the reason for this was that she disliked playing with boys and preferred the company of girls. Another *kathoey*, Neung, reported that from the age of eleven years she *'... started acting, everything, like the lady; want everything like the lady ...'*. Her older cousin, Tinar, also a *kathoey*, confirmed this: she remembered Neung *'... screaming like a girl, not fighting like a boy ...'*.

For the parents and families of other *kathoey* to whom I spoke, their child's *kathoey* status was obvious from a very young age, typically four to six years, having observed their 'boy' playing with 'dolls and girls'. Lek's narrative supports this. Asked whether, as a young child, Lek had told anybody that she was unhappy being a boy, she reported:

> *I had no need to tell; my Mum knew already. She saw me, looking like a lady. I do everything like a lady and my mother knew.*

Others, as noted above, reported having been dressed in their older sister's clothes as a small child, or spending a lot of time with the female members of the family while their fathers worked away, and that this was perhaps the rationalization as to why they turned out to be *kathoey*. It is interesting that while transgender in Thailand is understood in terms of Buddhism and *karma*, when I asked *kathoey* why they thought they were transgender, they rationalized it in other ways. As one *kathoey* in Bangkok reported:

> *Maybe I could not spend time with my Dad because he work*
> *away and I stay with my Mum and my two sisters. And*
> *sometimes I went to my aunt and my aunt got three daughters*

AB: *I see, so you were left with the girls?*

K: *Uh huh. And I am quite weak you know, I was not strong,*
> *so I cannot play with boys, you know, they play hard, I can't*
> *play with them, I don't like ...*

AB: *And did you tell anybody that you thought you were a girl?*

K: *I felt everyone knew .... They knew from my personality, you*
> *know, the way I behave ...*

The narrative of another *kathoey*, a graduate student, I have called 'Malee', goes some way to support the claim that physically 'weak' boys who are 'treated like girls' can develop into *kathoey*. Malee reported:

> *At home my parents treat me, sometimes, treat me as a girl*
> *because I am so [physically] weak. I seem to catch illness, easy*
> *to catch a cold ... my body quite little, small body ... but when*
> *I go to school, in my school they treat me like the other boys ...*

We have explored the experiences of transsexual women and *kathoey* as they discovered their transgender status and the coping mechanisms used to facilitate 'cross-dressing'. Now I would like to examine the 'coming out' stage experienced by informants of 'becoming' a virtual woman.

'Coming Out': England: "When the Genie comes out of the box..."

'Coming out' is a relatively new term commonly associated with homosexuality. The term 'coming out' implies a release from 'hiding' in some form of prison, whether that be a metaphorical closet, or as Marion termed it, a 'genie's box', or the prison of an emotional state or self identity, or to borrow Plummer's (2001, p.83) term: 'a different and shifting vision of Self', the 'challenge' being to 'find the *'real'* or *'authentic'* Self in the telling' (2001, p.87; emphasis added). And yet when that 'real' or 'authentic' Self is released, the new life *'... is not the "real" life, but the composed life...'* (2001, p.88).

A major difficulty that the British transsexual women of this study have had to face is the actual 'coming out' and the consequent fear of rejection by family and friends. Tanya explained:

> *It seemed such a big thing, well it did for me anyway, and it does for a lot of transsexuals, the transition, I mean how do you <u>begin</u> to tell people? And it feels like you have got this cliff face — and you look up and there is this massive height above and that is where you have got to be and you think, 'How the hell can I get there? How the hell can I do this?' But the reality is a big thing to do, but not as hard as you think it will be. And once you start doing it, it is a bit of a roller coaster of emotions ... [Underlining indicates emphasis in tone of voice].*

The gender dysphoric child in Western society very soon comes to realize the potential folly of revealing their 'difference' to parents, siblings, teachers, school friends, and the inevitable stigma that will ensue. Having discovered that the root of their distress lies in a so-called 'medical condition' known as 'gender dysphoria', they internalise the 'knowledge' of this difference and learn to conceal it in ways that they describe variously as 'masquerading as a male'; or efforts of presenting themselves as the 'standard issue bloke'; or as a 'pretty good impersonation of a male' and learn to live trapped in what Plummer (2001:94) terms: 'stigmatizing silence'. However, at some point the 'genie' has to 'come out of the box', as one informant, echoing the voices of others in this study, reported: '... *I couldn't carry on with this charade of trying to be a man ... I just coped with it as best as I could ...*'

Such descriptions of their former presentations of (the male) self serve to conjure up for the researcher a picture of hiding strategies, as the voices of the transsexual women aforementioned in this chapter testify, of 'burying' the true self-identity, or 'banking' the 'real' person behind a fraudulent 'male' persona that 'felt alien' to them. Others will find a strategy for expression of their essentially female self through autobiographical websites; 'personal websites in Cyberspace' (Plummer,

2001:100), 'cyber documents' (Plummer, 2001:96) authored in their female name, in a way that goes some significant way towards denial of the male.

For the transwoman, 'Coming out' means abandoning the male persona for a newly constructed female Self via *rites de passage* and a period of liminality (Turner, 1967), the 'Transition', that leads to the metamorphosed, integrated self in the life of the new (virtual) woman. In the next chapter I examine this very transition as seen through the eyes of the virtual women of this study. Firstly, though, let us examine the initial stage of that transition: 'coming out'.

The 'composed' lives of the British pre-operative transsexual women of this study, aware of the impossibility of the incongruence between their gender identity and their physicality, meant finding coping strategies by embarking upon careers that are stereotypically 'male-oriented' work, including the armed forces. As Gina explained:

> *I decided I was going to change my brain and be a man.*
> *I consciously set about stripping away what I perceived*
> *as feminine traits out of my mind and adopted the*
> *masculine role.*

To this end, Gina joined the Royal Air Force. This strategy of 'trying to make a man' of themselves, was common amongst the subjects of this study. Recall that Kate, also served in the Royal Air Force, while yet another informant, Caroline, joined the merchant navy[35] and served as a chief engineer. Tanya's strategy took the form of working as an engineer in the aviation business while her spare time was taken up by motorcycle racing. Gill spent many years working as an engineer offshore on oilrigs, and as

---

35 Indeed, famously, transsexual woman April Ashley, also joined the merchant navy in an attempt to 'make a man' of herself. She subsequently underwent sex reassignment surgery in Casablanca and married British aristocrat, Arthur Corbett. Applying to the court for the marriage to be annulled, Judge Ormrod ruled in Corbett's favour on the ground that Ashley was born male, and that this meant the marriage was unlawful, as it was between two genetic males. The Corbett v. Corbett case was to have serious legal consequences for transsexual people until the law changed and the Gender Recognition Act (2004) was enacted in April 2005.

one astute observer stated: 'What a great place to hide!' Other 'composed' lives included getting married and fathering children, in a bid to hide or bury their 'guilty secret', only to find that their gender dysphoria intensified rather than waned. Coming out, then, to wives and children, parents and siblings, perhaps unsurprisingly, generated anger, disbelief, revulsion in others, as well as great distress to not only the gender dysphoric person themselves, but their families also. Informants reported responses ranging from total shock, huge emotional distress[36] and disbelief to outrage and even violence. One informant described her wife's reaction to the news that her 'husband' was transsexual and intended to transition:

> ... *it was hellish, it was awful, I cannot describe how bad the conflict was... I had a carving knife drawn on me one night ... she got a carving knife out of the kitchen drawer and she said, "Come over here and do us both a favour".*

In this case, the wife's rage at discovering that her husband and father of her children was transsexual and intended to transition, was perhaps aggravated by the fact that she had entered the marriage oblivious to her husband's transgender status, and the discovery had left her feeling betrayed and denied 'the right to choose'. Gill recalled the emotional trauma of 'coming out' to her wife of 15 years, who had been totally unaware that her 'husband' cross-dressed, let alone was transsexual:

> ... *she was screaming and really angry with me and I just broke down completely, a total breakdown and I said, "OK, this is it, here's the truth" and I told her... and it all poured out, and I told her about the cross-dressing ...*

[Long pause as Gill is getting upset at the memory of it; I try to

---

36   One informant who reported that her teenage daughter refused point-blank to acknowledge that her father was becoming a woman, and coped with this by refusing to see her TS parent for years after she had transitioned, illustrates an example of this. The voices of the children, parents, spouses and other family members of transsexuals deserve to be heard; however, this is another research project and far outside of the scope of this book.

support her: 'It's OK, take your time, I can turn the tape off if you prefer, we don't have to continue if you'd rather not']

Gill composes herself; she continues:

> No, no, it's OK. And yes, everything came out. And she
> listened to me for an hour or so and she said, "OK; I can
> understand why you have hidden this ... but let's see what
> we can do about it ..."

At the time, however, Gill herself was unaware (being 'in denial', as she put it) that she was transsexual, and believed herself to be *just a cross-dresser*, as if that were somehow the 'lesser of the two evils'. Therefore, whilst Gill had 'come out' as a cross-dresser, it was a number of years before she reached what she termed 'the realization' of her true transgender status and was able to come out as being transsexual. This, for Gill, as well as for some of the other informants in this study, happened during a guided meditation at a 'spiritual retreat'. Here is what Gill had to say:

> ... it was just like this almighty big bomb going off, and it
> was just like, "Oh my god!" and it was from that point on
> that I started seeing all the pointers, all the things that I
> had hidden, you know, I had pushed them aside. And from
> that point, the conviction [to transition] just got stronger
> and stronger and stronger ... and people were saying to me,
> "you are going too fast, come on, slow down" and I was saying,
> "no, I know what I am doing" because the feeling was so
> strong, and it never waned, that strength, from that point.
> And it was like clicking a switch, from one person to another
> ... and that conviction just got stronger and stronger ...

Throughout our contact, Gill has maintained persuasively that it was what she calls her 'spirituality', together with the emotional support that she received from friends around her that enabled her to transition so comparatively easily. These facts, notwithstanding however, were coupled with the fact that Gill, a British transsexual woman, lived at that time in Thailand, where she was surrounded by her group of supportive expat and Thai friends, and where transgender does not carry with it the same generally negative response or social stigma as is often the case in Western society. Back in England, however, Gill's mother found the news of her coming out difficult to accept. Here is what Gill had to say :

> ... *my mother, she definitely went through a period of denial and she couldn't tell anybody... I implored her, "please, please talk to somebody ... talk to somebody professionally, who can put all this in perspective for you ..." and of course, she didn't, she kept it all bottled up for about twelve months ...*

However, at the time, Gill's mother had not yet met 'Gill'. Some time after this interview was carried out, I met Gill's mother, who had since met Gill and was now happy and accepting of her new daughter. She told me, '*who would have thought it, at my age* [84 years old] *— having a daughter'*.

Nicole's mother also found the news of her 'son's' transition to womanhood difficult to come to terms with. Fear of the unknown, together with fear for her child's health and wellbeing are difficult emotions to deal with. Nicole told me:

> *My mother, I told her ... and you know she was crying, she was upset, she was frightened, and I had all this stuff prepared for her to read... but she didn't want to read about it, she wanted to learn it naturally from me ... she has got to know through me.*

With respect to coming out to her father, here is what Nicole had to say:

> *My father ... indicated when I spoke to him on the phone that he had read a lot and knew all about it; but I reckon he has read bugger all, well his behaviour indicated that*

he has read bugger all, or he hasn't taken it in or taken it seriously, probably dismissed it as some pseudo-science stuff.

Another informant, Lucy, reported having tried to be 'open and honest' with her wife before getting married. However, her 'honesty' only went so far. Here is what she had to say:

> *The first time I told her [wife] we had been together twelve months ... I loved her and felt I needed to be honest with her. But I wasn't completely honest with her, I told her I had been cross-dressing, but that it was no more than that and I had learnt to control it ...*
>
> AB: *How did she react when you told her?*
>
> Lucy: *She said, "thank heaven, I thought you were going to tell me you were having an affair or you were gay".[37] [Lucy breathes a deep sigh of relief here].*

Despite Lucy's attempt at honesty and openness regarding her gender dysphoria, the marriage floundered and the couple divorced. Nevertheless, Lucy, full in the knowledge by this time that she was indeed transsexual and wished to live as a woman, was nonetheless still driven to find another 'life partner' and met a woman who proposed marriage :

> *She asked me to marry her three times, and ... the third time she asked I said yes. But three weeks before we got married I told her that I know I am transsexual that I had known since I was a child and I know I couldn't carry on living the way I was... and she says, "I can't marry you", and I was devastated ... and I was looking at her and she was in such pain and I felt guilty and I says, "I'll marry you, I won't do it, I'll stop dressing ..." because she'd helped me, she'd helped me to cross-dress, you know ...*

---

37 Similar responses were reported in this regard. Sonya, an English post-op transsexual woman I met in Thailand, reported 'coming out' to a close, platonic female friend, who was relieved upon hearing of her friend's trans-status, having thought that Sonya was perhaps going to ask her out!

Some wives, although fearful at their husband's disclosure of his cross-dressing that he might be transsexual, tried to facilitate the 'dressing'. Marion recalled the time that she revealed to her wife, Brenda that she had been cross-dressing. Marion explained:

> *... and then the first question she asked me was — the obvious one — "Look, this is only about wearing clothes, isn't it? This is not about wanting to be a woman?"*

As stated previously, Marion reported having been '*... still totally in denial...*' about her transsexual status, passing it off as '*just cross-dressing*', reassuring Brenda: '*Oh, no, no', you know, 'it is none of that ...*' However, as time went on, Brenda, having become aware of her husband's considerable emotional distress, urged 'him' to tell her. Marion went on:

> *... I started crying myself to sleep. I ... started to lose weight, I took a vertical drop into depression, and [Brenda] just said, "Look, for God's sake just tell me what it is" and I just said to her, "Look, it is the gender thing", and that was the first time I had told anyone ...*
> *[Marion gets tearful at this point and I wait for her to recover her composure].*

Marion continued:

> *... as you can imagine, there were an awful lot of tears ...*
> *AB:*   *Yes. It must have been such a shock for her.*
> *M:*   *Of course. And she had never really had any inkling and potentially it was the end of her world, just as potentially it was the end of mine [here Marion is alluding to her own suicidal thoughts] ... and she said, "Look, you have got to go and get some help".*

While Brenda had not been aware of Marion's transgender status, other informants coming out reported having family members revealing that they had suspected gender dysphoria for some time, and such revelation had come as a complete surprise for the transsexual. Hetti recalled coming out to her mother:

Hetti: ... until I had decided that I was going to transition, I never mentioned it to my parents. And once I decided that I was going to transition, then I knew I had to tell them ...

Hetti's mother admitted that she had always known her 'son' had a gender identity problem because she remembered having found items of her clothing secreted away in his wardrobe when he was a young child. Hetti continued:

> *My Mum, she already knew; she didn't know how deep it was, or whether I was transsexual or just transvestite or whatever, but she knew ...*
> *... And when I told her, I was crying, and she was saying all the things to me that really I should be saying to her. She knew I had been looking at photos of transsexuals and whatever and she had seen programmes [on television] and she knew all the ins and outs.*

In this chapter we have explored the various roads to 'becoming a woman' that transwomen in England and *kathoey* in Thailand travel in order to deal with their anomalous status as transgenders in their respective societies. I hope it has given you an insight into the enormity of the difficulties that transsexual people face on the road to transition. In the next chapter we can examine the crucial next stage in the trans-life: that of the transition from male to female.

CHAPTER FIVE

Living "Betwixt and Between"
The Transitional Journey to Virtual Womanhood

> *... transitional beings ... are neither one thing nor*
> *another; or may be both; or neither here nor there;*
> *... are at the very least "betwixt and between"...*
> Turner (1967, p.97).

Let us now take a look at the transitional journey to 'womanhood' and the two systems of transition operating in England and Thailand.

Transitioning in England

As discussed earlier in this book, transsexualism is a worldwide if comparatively rare phenomenon, which is classified as a psycho-medico problem in Western countries. Cultural variations to the transgender phenomenon and its multifarious expressions in different cultural contexts notwithstanding, transsexualism is understood in the Western sense as a condition in which the transsexual person typically experiences their morphological body as out of sync with their gender identity. As noted earlier, such a person is commonly (but perhaps erroneously) described as 'a woman trapped inside a man's body'. Indeed, as I have already alluded elsewhere in this book, some neuroscientific studies suggest that the male-to-female transsexual person is 'female in the brain' (Kruijver, 2004; Gooren, 1993; Zhou, et al, 1995) or even 'intersexed in the brain'[38]. Many transsexual individuals believe that the only solution to the intense discomfort that arises from the incongruence they experience between their gender identity and physicality is hormone therapy and sex reassignment surgery in order

---

38 I should make clear here, that 'in the brain' does not mean and is in no way the same as 'in the mind' or even 'all in the mind'; the former explains transsexualism as a result of an almost palpable, and certainly tangible, physical structure in the brain, whilst the latter explains transsexualism as something that can be 'cured' with psychiatric treatment, which it clearly cannot.

to bring the two as closely as possible into line with each other. To this end, the person who is a male-to-female transsexual in England is placed under the scrutiny of the psychiatric profession, and required to undergo protracted psychiatric assessment at a Gender Identity Clinic before the prescription of carefully controlled hormone treatments. Paradoxically, while gender dysphoria is, according to Western neurobiological research, a condition that is present at birth and is not classified as a 'mental' illness, the transsexual person is 'treated' by psychiatrists and cannot proceed for sex reassignment surgery on the NHS without lengthy psychiatric evaluations at a gender identity clinic. As Payer (1988/1996:155) notes, '... *most doctors ... continue to hide behind the screen of "scientific" medicine that somehow takes precedence over "unscientific" patient desires*.' What Payer terms 'cultural biases' dictate the method of treatment of transsexuals. In England this takes the form of a paternalistic, hegemonic gatekeeper system (in terms of medical autonomy), whereas in Thailand doctors take a more facilitating, patient-centred approach. It is perhaps useful at this juncture to consider the historical significance of the paternalistic nature of the medical profession operating in England.

'*Stuffing their mouths with gold*': The NHS and doctors' autonomy — a short historical note

Prior to the launch of the National Health Service in Britain in 1948, medical care was largely available only to those who could afford to pay (BMJ Editorial, 1998; BMA, 2006). Before the NHS was launched, Lloyd George had, in 1911, brought about the National Insurance Act; however, this only extended to workers (that is, specifically men, who were the main breadwinners). Women and children were excluded from free health care at the time, meaning that only those who could afford to pay could expect treatment from the doctor.

General practitioners' attitudes to patients differed in accordance with their ability or inability to pay. Rivett (1998) claims that they treated working class patients discourteously, while those who could afford to pay (that is, the middle-classes) were treated with respect. Rivett (1998, p.2) notes,

Successful treatment by the family doctor was accepted with gratitude and the many failures were tolerated without rancour or recrimination. Patients' expectations were not high.

Doctors, then, were placed in an elevated social space and revered by the community, irrespective as to whether patients were successfully 'cured' or whether they were treated with courtesy and respect in return. The doctor was automatically in command because he was perceived as the one holding the knowledge and the power to 'cure' the patient. As Freidson (1972, p.9) argues, through doctors' elevated occupational status, they have *'gained command of <u>exclusive competence</u> to determine the proper <u>content</u> and <u>effective method</u> of performing some task'* (emphasis mine). The medical profession, so as to show that the patient accepts the doctor as the one who has the knowledge and expertise to 'cure' them, lays down the 'rules' of medicine. Moreover, the doctor enjoys autonomy in ways that other professions do not. Indeed, some would argue that the only profession that is 'truly autonomous' (Friedson, 1970, p.136) is the medical profession. Such autonomy is maintained because of the expert knowledge of medicine that the doctor or consultant possesses (or is perceived as possessing). However, doctors also need the general public to believe (and so collude in the notion) that the doctor is the all-powerful font of medical knowledge and expertise. Hence the 'superior' status of the doctor is observed and upheld by the public. This is what Freidson (1972, p.12) refers to as the *'... cultural acceptability of the practices of a special occupational group* [viz., the medical profession] *to a receiving public.* Thus the general public have, historically, accepted the superiority of the doctor, whilst colluding in the maintenance of the upholding of that status quo. However, Freidson rightly argues that to reduce medical autonomy and dominance could *'... destroy the capacity of professionals to do their ... invaluable work properly'* (1970, p.234).

Thus, doctors have traditionally enjoyed autonomy but in the late 1940s feared this would be lost with the advent of the then Labour Government's Minister of Health, Nye Bevan's visionary National Health Service (NHS), where health care would be centralized and available to everyone, regardless of the ability to pay. The medical profession opposed the Government's proposal for a centralized and nationalized public health care system. Webster (1998/2002:3) notes that the changeover from the health services, in place prior to the Second World War, to the NHS system was '...*characterized by protracted and intense dispute*'. A centralized health care system, warned the British Medical Association (BMA), could jeopardize the profession's independence (BMJ Editorial, 1998). The BMA and the Labour Government 'spent many months of acrimonious and public confrontation' (BMJ Editorial, 1998). General practitioners and hospital doctors alike worried about the adverse effect of nationalizing voluntary hospitals and the loss of their influence in teaching hospitals. They were reluctant to lose the freedom that came with private practice, fearing it would 'convert them to salaried employees and compromise their clinical independence' (BMJ Editorial, 1998). The BMA held a plebiscite — a referendum — of all doctors that resulted in 75 percent of the medical profession opposing the Government's terms for the NHS. Nye Bevan, in co-operation with Lord Moran, (Winston Churchill's personal physician) struck a compromise whereby consultants who worked within the new NHS could retain their autonomy by being allowed to carry on treating private patients as well as NHS patients. Negotiations between Lord Moran and Bevan were well received, as in the event, 95 percent of the medical profession joined the NHS. Hence, Bevan famously stated that he had gained consultants' backing to implement the NHS by 'stuffing their mouths with gold' (BBC News, 1 July 1998; BMA, 2006).

The legacy of the private health care system in place prior to 1948 is that the medical profession's continuing patriarchal authority still prevails today. This autonomy has been reduced somewhat as a result of the health service reforms beginning in the Thatcher era and continuing to the present. However, despite the 'managerialism' introduced into the NHS, doctors still retain much clinical autonomy, as became evident from the interviews I carried out for this study. Indeed, Nettleton (1995:141) points to the argument put forward by radical feminists that 'modern medicine' is 'inherently patriarchal' and that such patriarchy is illustrated by the way that 'men have seized control over women's bodies'. The same patriarchal attitude applies to transsexual women's bodies, because as psychiatrists act as gatekeepers to surgery, they control the transitional journey of their patients. By bypassing the gatekeeper system and travelling to Thailand, transsexuals are taking back control over their own bodily destinies.

Transitioning on the NHS

The National Health Service has provided first class health care to a great many, not least those less fortunate than others. This chapter is not intended to denigrate the NHS in any way, but rather to present the experiences of the transsexual women who encounter what *they* see as an inadequate system of transition. While sex reassignment surgery is available in England on the NHS, this route necessarily involves protracted waiting time and any recommendation for surgery is dependent upon the transsexual patient's successful completion of a 'real life test' or 'real life experience' as it is now more commonly referred to. In England, the real life experience involves living and working full-time in the female role (in the case of the person transitioning from male-to-female) for a number of years whilst undergoing lengthy psychiatric/psychotherapeutic treatment or assessment. The real life experience has to be commenced and evaluated before hormones are prescribed. In England, then, the transsexual person is faced with a 'gatekeeper' system that carefully monitors the transitioning process, but even then, sex reassignment surgery on the NHS is not guaranteed. However, the general feeling amongst the 'professional' gatekeepers is that the real life experience is vital to the satisfactory outcome of the transition. One psychiatrist put it like this:

> *I think there is sense in living as a woman, you know, before you go the whole hog. Equally, if you have got no breasts it is not easy, but people do manage it and I don't think it is unreasonable to say you should give it a go before you have the operation, rather than say that once you've had the operation it will all come naturally. It might to some, but I think that a lot of [trans]people need to have worked through that.*

Another psychiatrist, working at a Gender Identity Clinic reported that the length of transition 'depends on the state of play' at the time of the first appointment. He reported that it could be as short as a year or less if the person has already lived in the female role for a long time. Changing role as from the first appointment meant that transition could be two and a half years if the person changed role at arrival. However, he estimated that the average transitioning period might be three and a half years. As we shall find in this chapter, at least one transwoman (Kelly) in this study waited over six years, only to give up and, like many other transsexual women, she travelled to Thailand for surgery.

A psychiatrist at one Gender Identity Clinic confirmed that hormones are only given when the patient has either already changed gender role (that is, having commenced the 'real life experience'), or after at least six months of psychotherapy. More commonly it is the former rather than the latter, and this was an issue that caused great distress to many of the transwomen of this study, who had started the transitioning process on the NHS. However, the prescription of hormones is subject to there being no contraindications to their use. This same psychiatrist rightly warned of the dangers of patients undertaking hormone treatment without medical supervision, as was the case reported by some transsexual informants of this study, as well as undergoing sex reassignment surgery without having carried out a 'real life experience'. He explained,

> If people take hormones without changing [gender] role, they may do so for years, exposed to medical risks, and with no obvious benefit. Surgery without prior role change is a disaster. One person had thousands of pounds of surgery, GRS [genital or gender reassignment surgery; an alternative term for sex reassignment surgery], implants, the lot — in Thailand. On return to the UK she found she still could not pass as a woman. It takes more than how you look. This person shelled out a lot more here in UK to have as much reversed as could be reversed.

On the issue of the length of time of the 'real life experience', psychiatrists seem to differ in their opinions. For example, while one Gender Identity Clinic psychiatrist was quite clear in his view that the 'real life experience' is a crucial part of the transitioning process another psychiatrist held that while it is necessary, there should be some flexibility in this regard. Here is what he had to say:

> ... I think there is a lot to be said for having established yourself as a woman beforehand, but whether it has to be for two years and whether it has to be so severe, I have my doubts. I do it on an individual basis, frankly. Personally, if you look at people who have done two years, some of them were managing quite well after one year... I mean, [names one Gender identity Clinic] want it [the 'real life experience'] and I sort of do my best to help people go along with it ...

From a patient-centred approach, however, having to carry out the 'real life experience' without the aid of hormones is extremely distressing. It means having to shave the face and other male-pattern hair growth on the body, before applying makeup, a wig (as many such people are so maturely masculine that they suffer male-pattern baldness), female clothes and going to work so attired. Caucasian transsexual women need the effects of hormones to aid in feminizing changes to the body, to enable them to start the real life experience. The ingestion of female hormones (oestrogens) serves to encourage the development of female bodily characteristics such as breast growth, larger hips and thighs, and smaller waist. Other cosmetic treatments are also necessary but the cost of much of this must be borne by the patient. Typically, this includes a procedure known as Thyroid Chondroplasty that reduces the 'Adam's apple', and electrolysis or laser treatment to remove facial and other characteristically male pattern bodily hair. Speech therapy is frequently necessary to help soften and develop a female voice pitch. Some transwomen choose to undergo vocal cord stretching to assist in the feminizing of the voice by raising the vocal register to a higher pitch. Although the breasts will usually develop following the ingestion of oestrogen, some transsexual women will undergo breast surgery (silicone or saline implants) to create larger breasts. Facial feminization surgery can be carried out, for example, brow reduction or rhinoplasty to 'feminize' the nose, making it shorter and narrower. Finally, genital surgery completes the transition.

"Behave Yourself!"
The Gender Identity Clinic as a Goffmanesque Total Institution

Now that we have looked at what transsexual women try to achieve through surgical technology, let us examine the process of this achievement. Typically the psychiatrist, having diagnosed transsexualism, will require the transsexual patient to attend a Gender Identity Clinic on a regular basis for assessment. A Gender Identity Clinic can serve a wide catchment area, meaning that many patients have long journeys to travel for appointments.

It seems to me that the Gender Identity Clinic operates in a way that echoes sociologist Irving Goffman's *Asylums* (1968), in that it treats transsexual clients as 'mental patients'. In his book, Goffman describes the study of the universal model of an American State psychiatric hospital in the 1950s, where the authority of the attendant (or the psychiatric nurse) is reinforced by positive and negative power that serves to control the patients. Control comes in the form of privileges and punishment. Among the list of privileges is the treatment by doctors and nurses of 'good' or 'well-behaved' patients with 'personal kindness and respect' (Goffman, citing Belknap, 1968, p.54). Like Goffman's 'total institution', the rules of the Gender Identity Clinic serve to humiliate the patient, while stripping away the 'old' self, making way for the 'new' self (except, of course, that in the case of the transsexual 'patient', this process is to some extent, voluntary).

In Goffman's asylum, the total institution is authority directed. The 'dress', 'deportment' and 'manners' of the inmate are constantly judged as signs of whether the patient's mental health is improving. Some of the transsexual women of this study, with personal experience of treatment at a Gender Identity Clinic have reported what, I would contend, are parallels with the Goffmanesque model of total institutions and the treatment or control of psychiatric patients as described by Goffman. For example, the hegemony that prevails and the attitude of some psychiatrists means that they have absolute power over the transsexual 'patient' attending the Gender Identity Clinic on the NHS. The Gender Identity Clinic has a set of rules (or, as some of the transsexual women of this study have termed it, 'jumping through loops'), and any deviance from the criteria as laid down by the psychiatrist can result in the threat of withholding 'treatment' or sex reassignment surgery. Transsexual informants of this study, who had started their transition on the NHS, reported that when attending a Gender Identity Clinic, strict rules of dress code apply; for example, the patient is expected to present themselves *'en femme'* and attire must include a skirt or dress rather than jeans or trousers, and the overall presentation is required to be in keeping with some notion of the 'feminine'. For the transsexual person attending the Gender Identity Clinic, the dress, deportment and 'feminine' demeanour are judged by the psychiatrist, and serve as an insignia as to whether or not she is likely to graduate to a convincingly 'feminine woman'. The Gender Identity Clinic, then, becomes a kind of 'Finishing School' for transsexual women. It is noteworthy that, while the concept of 'femininity' is highly subjective and variant, in the case of the transsexual woman it is defined according to the personal opinion of the psychiatrist as to what is and what is not 'feminine'[39]. The rationale behind this practice is to enable the psychiatrist to assess the likelihood of the transsexual patient's success at living 'in role', as a woman, on a permanent basis, and to this end, the transsexual person is then required to undergo the 'real life experience'. In the asylum, as Goffman's notes, *'rewards and privileges are held out in exchange for obedience to staff ...'* (1968, p.51). Punishment can take many forms, including the 'suspension of all privileges', or 'withholding access to professional personnel' (1968, p.54). One transwoman I spoke to attended a Gender Identity Clinic wearing jeans, along with a feminine top and accessories. On seeing her, the psychiatrist voiced

---

39 A consultant psychiatrist once described to me a transsexual woman patient, whose *'en femme'* dress sense he judged to be unsophisticated, as looking like a 'dog's breakfast'.

his disapproval that she was not wearing a skirt, reportedly saying, *'How do you expect me to take you seriously as a woman when you come here wearing jeans?'*. For the transsexual woman attending the Gender Identity Clinic, failure to adhere to the requirements of the real life experience can result in 'punishment' in the form of a deferment of the psychiatrist's referral for hormones or surgery.

It seems to me that along with the Goffmanesque aspects of NHS treatment of transsexual patients discussed above, that the character of the treatment for transsexualism is connected with the cultural and intrinsic peculiarities and paternalism of the British medical profession. In Thailand, as we will discover, the attitude of the health professionals is far less paternalistic and more patient-centred. However, access to the medical profession is available only to a limited number: those who can afford to pay.

Transitioning in Thailand

For the *kathoey* transitioning from male to female, the picture is a very different one. For the Thai *kathoey*, hormones can be easily bought, without prescription, over the counter in a pharmacy, and sex reassignment surgery is readily available with no 'gatekeeper' system to negotiate. Young *kathoey* are apparently unaware of unwanted side effects that ingesting female hormones can produce. Whereas in England the private body is treated as state property to be controlled by the medical establishment, in Thailand the body is 'owned' by the individual who is afforded jurisdiction over it, as long as they can afford it, even if that individual is a pubescent boy.

A growing number of British transsexual women bypass the 'gatekeeper' system in England and travel to Thailand for sex reassignment surgery and related surgeries performed by surgeons who are perceived as highly experienced due to the many *kathoey* upon whom they operate. For the transsexual patient travelling to Thailand and paying for sex reassignment surgery themselves is an attractive option that works out cheaper than private treatment in England and is certainly speedier and therefore preferable to the long NHS waiting lists and gatekeeper system that prevails in the UK. Another reason for British transsexuals going to Thailand for surgery is the results. Thai surgeons are believed by transsexual patients to be more experienced and their surgical techniques more sophisticated than those of their Western counterparts, and therefore aesthetically more convincing, and this is a very important concern from the subjective viewpoint of the transwoman. However, a common theme that emerged from the British sample of these data was the dissatisfaction they felt with the system in England, and in particular, what they viewed as the patriarchal and paternalistic attitude of psychiatrists at Gender identity Clinics, and this contrasted markedly with the respect and courtesy they experienced from Thai surgeons.

The relative ease with which *kathoey* are able to follow their own chosen transgendered path, and the comparatively high level of (at least tacit) social acceptance in Thailand sits in stark contrast to the life experiences of transsexual women in England. In England, the gatekeeper system with its lengthy road to transition and the somewhat paternalistic attitude of psychiatrists in gender identity clinics means that increasing numbers of British transwomen are opting for the swifter and easier option of going to Thailand. The point of highlighting the situation in Thailand is to illustrate that these young 'boys' who turn themselves into 'Ladyboys', as well as other Thai 'boys' who are actually transsexual, ('female in the brain') happen to live in a society which enables them to decide for themselves what they do with their own gendered bodies. One would contend that in the strictly regulated British 'gatekeeper' system, the body becomes, metaphorically, the 'property' of a society that allows transsexual people no jurisdiction over their own bodies. This also has to do with the centralised and public health care system (the NHS) that operates in England. In Thailand, the picture is a very different one. The question is, however, does the Thai system offer a safe alternative to the strictly controlled system of England? If transsexualism/gender dysphoria is psycho-pathologized in England, then this means that funding for sex reassignment surgery can be obtained on the NHS, albeit this involves long waiting lists and 'jumping through loops'. However, the dilemma is this: by not categorizing transsexualism/gender dysphoria as a 'medical/mental' condition those afflicted surely risk 'treatment' on the NHS being withheld. Paradoxically, then, British transsexuals have to collude in the 'medical model' that pathologizes transsexualism in order that they may take the NHS route to surgery. On the question of age differences between transitioning transsexual women in England and *kathoey* in Thailand, even though transsexualism and sex reassignment surgery are now widely known, as we see elsewhere in this book, transsexual women in England are still reticent about 'coming out', for fear of the inevitable stigmatization and possible ridicule they feel is sure to follow. After transition, transsexual women in England and *kathoey* in Thailand find they are not accepted in many aspects of society.

I've changed my mind...

The transitional journey is long, circuitous and rocky. Gender migration like geographical migration, is perceived as a one-way journey, with no going back. 'Sex change' operations are major surgeries. Moreover, such surgeries are virtually irreversible. However, there are some individuals who regret crossing the gender border and seek to return to their original gender classification. One psychiatrist at a Gender Identity Clinic argues that this is a very good reason for lengthy psychiatric treatment and the 'real life experience'. As he told me: *'Surgery without living in role is a disaster'*. However, as I have illustrated in these chapters, some transsexual women undergoing transition on the NHS find the regime and attitude of psychiatrists at the Gender Identity Clinic intolerable and this is one reason they give up and go to Thailand for treatment. This is, surely, an issue that needs to be addressed by the Gender Identity Clinics in UK.

The danger of post-operative regret lies, it seems to me, in the strategies adopted by transsexuals to ensure treatment. As Nicole and a transwoman gender counsellor I interviewed both told me, individuals seeking gender reassignment learn the 'script' of the typical 'transsexual story' and reproduce it for the psychiatrist in order to get treatment. If it is felt that a person is not a good candidate the psychiatric profession will delay or even withhold treatment and this is another reason that drives such people to give up on the British system and go to Thailand. I asked a psychiatrist at a Gender Identity Clinic, what happened to those transsexuals who 'failed' their 'real life experience'. Here is what he told me:

Those who 'fail' the RLE get long conversations with us about why it's not working. If it continues not to work they kind of figure out with us why not, and we think about whether other options will help. These might include changes of occupation, appearance, ways of interacting with others, or maybe a dual role transvestite lifestyle is going to suit better, or that of a very un-masculine man or unfeminine women. Only a very few remain chronically unsatisfied and saying that they are not 'getting what they want.'

I met British patients undergoing sex reassignment surgery in Thailand, who, on their own admission, would have not succeeded on the NHS and, subjectivities notwithstanding, I could not help but to see the reasons why. However, despite what the Thai surgeons reported to me, the researcher, such candidates for surgery found a Thai surgeon easier to convince of their 'true' transsexual status than was the case in England.

Stories have appeared in the British press of individuals who regretted undergoing sex reassignment surgery and wanted to change back to their original gender role (for example, Batty, 2004; Hardy, 2004). Such a situation is fraught with complexities, not least because it involves further major surgeries and an outcome that is at best a compromise, but at worst results in a life of misery and lonely isolation, as the person concerned finds the possibility of a 'meaningful' relationship unattainable. One such person was quoted as stating, *'I am not a woman, I am a thing'* (Batty, 2004).

Quite evidently, then, it is crucial that a stringent procedure of transition is in place to ensure, as far as possible, that the person migrating from one gender to another is not making an irreversible mistake. Clearly, the consequences of transitioning in error are monumental. It is for these reasons that the attitudes of psychiatrists at gender identity clinics that are complained about by transsexual patients needs to be addressed fully. By treating patients insensitively and with a patriarchal approach rather than a patient-centred, more facilitating approach, surely such catastrophic mistakes would be less likely to occur, when patients become disillusioned and frustrated and travel to Thailand for surgery before they are, incontrovertibly, ready for it.

Plates

19TH CENTURY SIAMESE KATHOEY 'ACTRESSES' RELAXING OFF-STAGE

A SIAMESE WOMAN IN THE LATE 19TH CENTURY. NOTE HER APPEARANCE IS
STRIKINGLY SIMILAR TO THAT OF THE KATHOEY ACTRESSES OF THE TIME

19TH CENTURY KATHOEY DANCERS

A KATHOEY WORKING IN A BANGKOK LADYBOY BAR

MISS ALCAZAR AND MISS TIFFANY, PATTAYA, 2004
(PHOTO COURTESY OF MISS PREMPREEDA PRAMOJNA AYYUTTAYA)

BLENDING GENDERS: MISS ACDC, MISS TIFFANY, MISS ALCAZAR, 2004
(PHOTO COURTESY OF MISS PREMPREEDA PRAMOJNA AYYUTTAYA)

MISS TIFFANY AND MISS ALCAZAR, PATTAYA 2004 (PHOTO COURTESY OF
MISS PREMPREEDA PRAMOJNA AYYUTTAYA)

KATHOEY CABARET BAR, PATTAYA

GILL
(CHAPTER 6 'GILL'S STORY' - PHOTO COURTESY OF MS GILL DALTON)

GILL
(PHOTO COURTESY OF MS GILL DALTON)

CHAPTER SIX
Gill's Story

By way of comparison to the transitioning journey transwomen in England and *kathoey* in Thailand, let me now tell you Gill's story. Gill, formerly known as 'Peter', is a British transsexual woman who had lived and worked in Thailand for some thirteen years when, what she termed, the 'realization' occurred to her that she was transsexual and needed to transition. Having identified herself as a 'secret cross-dresser' for all of her adult life, she decided to do nothing for one month after her 'realization', in order to give herself time to seriously consider exactly what transitioning would mean and involve.

After one month Gill set about researching hospitals to find an endocrinologist, having learned from previous research that the first step, as far as physical changes were concerned, would be to start on hormones. Gill felt she needed to find an endocrinologist with whom she could talk it through and be advised as to what the next step would be for her to transition in Thailand, and to this end consulted a senior endocrinologist at a Bangkok hospital. The appointment with him lasted ninety minutes while Gill gave him a full history and explained the circumstances that had led her to the point of consultation. This endocrinologist carried out in-depth questioning pertinent to her case and gave an explanation of the transitioning procedure to follow. This entailed prescribing hormones, advising her of the length of time she needed to take hormones before being considered suitable for surgery, and required her to attend within two weeks of commencement of hormones for a blood test. (Notably, Gill's endocrinologist monitored her hormone treatment, thus avoiding the need to buy the drugs over-the-counter, as do pubescent *kathoey*.) The first blood test was used by the doctor as a benchmark for the measurement of future hormone levels. Organ functions were assessed, as well as blood sugar levels to ensure that there were no physical or medical problems present and that she was physically fit to undergo transition. She attended regular monthly appointments with the endocrinologist, when she reported to him any physical changes that had occurred and stated that the endocrinologist's role also involved counselling her. This enabled him to evaluate any emotional implications that might have arisen from the effects of the hormones. Every second month blood tests were taken to check hormone levels and the dosage changed according to the results of these tests.

Since first consulting the endocrinologist Gill continued to work full time as a petroleum engineer based in Bangkok and the decision as to when she wanted to 'dress' and go out was in accordance with her own personal choice. She was not required to undergo a 'real life test' in order for hormones to be prescribed. In her working life, however, she always presented as 'male' because she was working in a male-oriented job. In stark contrast to the requirement of the gender identity clinic in England, for appointments with her doctor, Gill dressed in either male or female attire, according to her preference on the day.

Some months after commencement of hormone treatment, Gill asked the endocrinologist about the possibility of consulting a psychiatrist, having learned of the requirement for psychiatric evaluation from her own research. According to Gill, her endocrinologist informed her that while such assessment was a requirement, the decision as to when it should take place was entirely her own. An appointment for Gill to see a psychiatrist at the same hospital was made one week later.

For the consultation with the psychiatrist, mode of dress (masculine or feminine attire) was optional, but Gill recalled that she 'probably was dressed' *en femme*. The consultation lasted ninety minutes in which time Gill explained her history and how she had arrived at her decision to transition and get started on hormones. Gill recalled the psychiatrist having asked 'a lot of questions about history and family' and that this was 'quite in-depth'. Unlike some transsexual women's experience at Gender Identity Clinics in England, Gill was not asked about her 'sexual fantasies' although she was asked if she had ever been sexually attracted to men. Gill recalled that this was done with the greatest of sensitivity, unlike the subjective view that others expressed regarding their treatment at gender identity clinics in England. At the end of the appointment, according to Gill, the psychiatrist expressed the opinion that she was a 'perfect candidate' for sex reassignment surgery and his evaluation of her transition was that it would be successful. In Gill's own words, she would come through the transition with 'flying colours' and that he could not envisage her having 'any problems whatsoever'. He also went on to say that if she felt she needed to see him again, he was happy to see her, however, in his opinion this would not be necessary. She carried on with the hormones, the regular blood tests and appointments with the endocrinologist for some months before quitting her job and living full time as 'Gill'. The timing of this was in accordance with Gill's own choice, and not a requirement of her doctors. Unlike the regime in England, at no stage did any of her doctors state that they required Gill to be working and living full time as a woman.

Six months after her first decision to transition, Gill decided that she was ready to start having surgical procedures to feminise her appearance. These procedures were carried out at a different hospital where a highly experienced surgeon working in that area of expertise practised. The procedures involved: Adam's apple reduction as well as a procedure to stretch the vocal chords; a 'half face lift' to remove fat under neck and saggy jowl, and further surgery to feminize her nose.

Gill reported that before commencement of these procedures, she was required to see a psychiatrist at the hospital because sex reassignment procedures are virtually irreversible and the rationale behind this requirement was that she needed counselling to ensure she was making the right decision. She reported that the second psychiatrist had no knowledge of the first psychiatric report, but, notably, his evaluation mirrored that of the first psychiatrist. This appointment also lasted ninety minutes and the psychiatrist's advice to Gill was the same as that of the first evaluating psychiatrist.

Two months after the first surgical procedures were carried out Gill again consulted her endocrinologist. Her hormone levels had balanced and Gill asked the doctor when she could go ahead with genital surgery. Her hormone levels were acceptable and the endocrinologist evaluated her as ready for sex reassignment surgery, which was carried out in Bangkok approximately four months later. The time frame for all aspects of transition was, in contrast to the experiences of transsexual women's treatment in England, entirely in accordance with Gill's 'own choice'. All treatment was private and self-funded by Gill, as her medical insurance did not cover sex reassignment surgery or related surgeries. The total cost was approximately £9000 (in 2003) including genital surgery and all other surgical procedures. There were no post-operative complications. Post-operative care included checkups with her surgeon and endocrinologist, with satisfactory results in both cases. Within three weeks of surgery blood tests carried out to check hormone levels were satisfactory. Hormones were then reduced in dosage to minimum maintenance levels.

Unlike the stories of the other British transsexuals of this study, Gill reported that at no time did she feel 'intimidated', 'rushed', 'dismissed', 'infantilised' or 'humiliated' during all contact with medical professionals. She claimed to have been treated with respect and courtesy throughout and reported having felt 'cared for' and given as much time as she needed, never demeaned, and never 'told' what to do. She was 'advised' what steps would need to be taken, and when, but decisions were her own.

Are there lessons to be learned here? Let me take you back to Thailand now, to examine the work of Thai sex reassignment surgeons...

CHAPTER SEVEN
Thailand's Surgical Industry

In Thailand, a patriarchal 'gatekeeper' system is less dominant. I interviewed four Thai surgeons, two of whom were urologists and two plastic surgeons, all with varying degrees of experience of performing sex reassignment surgery on Thai *kathoey* as well as international patients. The first surgeon, whom I shall call Dr W, reported that as he does not consider transsexualism to be either a somatic disease or a psychiatric problem, he does not usually require his *kathoey* patients to have a psychiatric assessment, although on the rare occasion that he might suspect that a case is not a suitable candidate for sex reassignment surgery *('... that she is not sure that this is a real woman inside or not'),* he will require her to undergo psychiatric assessment before he will operate, sometimes imposing a delay for surgery until he feels certain in his mind that this is the right decision. In keeping with the other three surgeons I interviewed, Dr W requires a general health check, including HIV/AIDS tests to be carried out before surgery. The minimum age for sex reassignment surgery is, Dr W informed me, twenty. Indeed, all four surgeons told me the minimum age for surgery is twenty. However, as we learned from Lek's story (and indeed other *kathoey* I interviewed) sex reassignment surgery is, in practice, carried out routinely on patients considerably younger than twenty, without parental consent.

Dr W reported that in accordance with Harry Benjamin Guidelines for Standards of Care, he requires all of his Western transsexual patients to have undergone the 'real life experience' in their own countries. However, because his Thai candidates for sex reassignment surgery have already been living in the female role since a very young age, this criterion does not apply. As one surgeon pointed out, *'kathoey carry out their own real life test — it is what they do all their lives'.* Indeed, some of his Thai patients who consulted him for sex reassignment surgery are, he states, 'an over-indication' when compared to the Harry Benjamin Guidelines. Dr W reported that with some *kathoey* it is difficult for him to differentiate them from genetic women, because they have been taking female hormones since the age of ten. According to Dr W, transgender in Thailand is not considered 'abnormal' or 'psycho-pathological', but merely 'a little bit different' from the 'norm'.

The second surgeon interviewed, I shall call Dr T. A consultant urologist, Dr T requires of his patients, as noted above, a pre-operative health check, including HIV/AIDS test are compulsory. If the patient refuses, the surgery cannot go ahead; however, Dr T commented that if he refused to operate, the patient would merely go elsewhere. All of his patients consulting him for sex reassignment surgery are required to be a minimum age of twenty years. Those under the age of twenty require parental consent. A report of psychological assessment is required. Dr T reported that, in his opinion, psychiatric assessment before sex reassignment surgery is absolutely necessary to eliminate the possibility of psychiatric disorder. He told me:

> *Maybe some people have psychiatric problem, and if you don't do a psychiatric assessment, then you have got a problem; because I am a specialist in surgery, not in psychiatry. So I think it is very, very necessary.*

It is noteworthy that Dr T considers transsexualism to be of genetic origin, because it cannot be 'cured' by psychiatric treatment. Indeed, Professor Richard Green, formerly head of a Gender Identity Clinic in England, accepts that psychiatry cannot 'cure' transsexualism.

The third surgeon, Dr J, is a consultant urologist in a Bangkok hospital. He reported having worked in the field of sex reassignment surgery for thirty years and proudly claimed to have carried out 'almost 600' operations. He had a novel and somewhat quirky strategy for assessing a patient's degree of femininity. I asked him if he required his patients to do a 'real life test', as is the case in the West:

> *No, no, we don't do this kind of thing, no ... We just do a simple test, you know ... When I interview them, I give them two handkerchiefs, one is for the female, one for the*

> *male, and say, 'OK, you wipe off your sweat', and most of*
> *the transsexual, they use the female handkerchief.*
>
> AB: *Really?*
>
> Dr J: *Yes, and some of them, I am looking for the panties. Most*
> *of the transsexual, they use the female panties.*

Dr J reported that the minimum age requirement is twenty, and the oldest patient he had performed sex reassignment surgery on was a fifty-two-year-old Westerner. *Kathoey* patients fall within the twenty to thirty year age range, according to Dr J, although he added that he had rarely come across a *kathoey* past the age of thirty, indicating that age is a significant dimension in the case of the Thai *kathoey*. I asked him if he believed that pre-operative psychiatric assessment was absolutely necessary; his answer makes interesting food for thought. Here is what he had to say:

> *It is, but now most of the psychiatrists, they refuse to look*
> *after these people, they do, most of the Thai psychiatrists they*
> *say it is investing too much time in these people ... only a*
> *few of them, they give time, for a little variation ...*

Significantly, Dr J opined that transsexuality is a psychological disorder. He continued:

> *... most of them need to visit a psychiatrist, even though most*
> *of the psychiatrists are not happy to do that.*

Finally, Dr H was interviewed. Dr H is a plastic surgeon whose patients come as referrals from endocrinologists or psychiatrists, and he has a growing number of Western candidates for sex reassignment surgery who find him via his website. Dr H requires a psychiatric certificate from his Western patients and the usual routine health checks and HIV/AIDS tests from all his patients. I asked him if he required *kathoey* patients to see a psychiatrist. Here is what he had to say:

Not really, in Thailand, no — this is a good question, not
the same as in the western patient who come to have surgery
in Thailand because as we talked before, if you see a Ladyboy,
maybe the most of them are the typical characteristic of the
female, and we know that she is transsexual, so I think in
practice they do need the reference from psychiatrist, but
the psychiatrist's evaluation may not be so strict ... or not
have such a long period that it is in the West ...

AB: *... so do you need a certificate from the psychiatrist?*
Dr H: *For those that come from the West, yes.*

Dr H feels that there are some Western patients who are not good candidates for sex reassignment surgery, and for this reason he claims he is careful to ensure they are all psychiatrically assessed before they travel to Thailand for surgery:

Even if they come with the [psychiatric] certificate, I think
when I interview, I notice ... she maybe have a mental problem
... Because I worry, you know, that the condition we call a
psychosis or schizophrenia may be, like, what you call, disorder;
they can change their mind later, and this is very dangerous.

Dr H sets a lower age limit of minimal twenty years, maximum sixty-five years of age. Under eighteen years of age he absolutely refuses surgery. However, if a patient is aged between eighteen and twenty years, he requires parental consent. According to Dr H, the same criteria applies to both Thai and western patients; however, for Thais the criteria are 'more flexible'. Asked if he would ever operate on a patient who had not undergone psychiatric assessment, Dr H had this to say:

Dr H: *Never, because we know that this is a surgery that is*
       irreversible. If you miss ... a psychosis ... you have a big
       problem, they might change their mind, something like that.
AB: *So your set of criteria is really quite stringent, isn't it, for*
       accepting a patient for sex reassignment surgery?

Dr H: Yes, but you know we need to have criteria for psychiatrically assessing the patient, because if they passed psychological evaluation, for one psychiatrist, I think in Thailand this is OK, but for the Western patient, I am not sure, maybe they need to have two psychiatrists to re-check ... there is some flexibility.

Significantly, Dr H believes that transsexualism is 'sporadic' in that it seems to be a condition that appears only in isolated instances or locations and may be caused by mixed factors: genetic, congenital, pre-natal environmental (in the womb), and post-natal environmental. Such an explanation fails, however, to account for the relatively high numbers of kathoey evident in Thailand.

One explanation might be that, as kathoey are fully aware of the relative ease with which they can undergo sex reassignment surgery, that this encourages them to take to the surgeon's scalpel. It is my understanding that surgeons charge less to operate on kathoey than the fees they charge international patients. However, whether one is a relatively affluent Westerner or a kathoey from a poor background, the surgeons' fees have to be met.

Let us take a look, in the next chapter, at some of the ways that the funds are raised for surgeries by both kathoey and farang patients.

CHAPTER EIGHT

"I used to own a yacht — but I traded it in for a vagina!"

Sociologist Richard Ekins (1997, p.152) tells us of the experience of Gail, a transwoman who funded her sex reassignment surgery from an out of court settlement she received for unfair dismissal from employers who had first moved her into another office, then dismissed her from her job. The stories of some of the transwomen I spoke to echo Gail's story. Lawsuits brought before the courts by transwomen, included cases of unfair dismissal from employment, and the 'out of court' financial settlement enabled the transsexual plaintiff to pay for private sex reassignment surgery either in England (one case) or in Thailand. As highlighted in the epigraph to this chapter, one transwoman I met told me she sold her yacht to fund her sex reassignment surgery, while others raided their credit cards. Commonly, transwomen reported being heavily in debt as a result of the costs of transitioning. One transwoman sold her home and ended up living in a hostel after her surgery. Two English informants reported having worked as prostitutes to save up for sex reassignment surgery. One such informant reported that she raised the money for surgery in this manner. A friend had helped her to set herself up in an apartment as a 'call girl', and she reported this was a very lucrative, albeit an unsavoury and sometimes dangerous way of earning money. This informant told me she had been 'brutally raped' by a 'number of clients', although clearly I cannot corroborate this story. Being raped by one client is unfortunate; being raped by 'a number of clients' is perhaps a little less believable and made me wonder, I have to admit, whether I was being told an embellished story for dramatic effect. Another British transwoman that I met in Thailand told me her story of working for several years as a 'dominatrix' and that this was her sole source of income and funding for sex reassignment surgery. Other transwomen had enjoyed highly paid employment in predominantly 'male-oriented' jobs, and accordingly were able to afford sex reassignment surgery due to their high earnings. Others, like Nicole discussed in an earlier chapter, re-mortgaged their homes to raise the money for surgery. *Kathoey* raise funds in a variety of ways ...

Kathoey

'He fights like a man so he can become a woman[40]

Perhaps the most poignant story of a *kathoey*'s efforts to raise funds for surgery is that of kick-boxing champion, 'Norng Toom'. The film, 'Beautiful Boxer' (directed by Ekachai Uekrongtham, 2003) portrays the life story of *kathoey* kick-boxer (*'Muay Thai'*) Parinya 'Norng Toom' Jaroenphon, who was born into a poor family in Bangkok but grew up in Chiang Mai from the age of seven. Although his parents accepted him as a *kathoey*, as a young 'effeminate' boy, Norng Toom was reputedly often the victim of taunts and bullying by other boys, and it was one such occasion, when the bully challenged him to a round of kick-boxing, that the young *kathoey* first entered the ring, knocking out his opponent allegedly in three kicks. However, caution should be exercised when analysing such stories. We need to bear in mind that the film is being 'sold' to a public audience, and that such stories are more likely to attract box office sales than a story of a *kathoey* who grew up, as is most likely the case, in an environment where her 'difference' was accepted by family, friends and school. With the exception of Pui, no *kathoey* I met reported having been treated abusively as a child due to her transgender status.

'Norng Toom' went on to study the art of Thai kick-boxing with Muay Thai Master Kroo Arkom. As a sixteen- year-old, pre-op transsexual Norng Toom entered the ring at Lumpani Boxing Stadium in northern Thailand and, wearing red lipstick, makeup and 'his' long hair tied back, won twenty-two professional fights, eighteen of which were knockouts. Although Norng Toom's motivation to enter the boxing ring came from 'his' cultural and familial responsibility to help support 'his' parents and siblings, the prize money 'he' earned also enabled 'him' to pay for sex reassignment surgery (Veena & Parinyaporn, 2003). After Norng Toom had undergone sex reassignment surgery in 1999 at the age of nineteen, she continued her career as a kick-boxer, entering women's contests at temple (*'Wat'*) fairs and demonstrations.

---

40 Poster advertising the film, 'Beautiful Boxer', released in Bangkok, December, 2003.

Nadia's story

In Thailand, perhaps unsurprisingly, some *kathoey* reported having funded sex reassignment surgery with money earned through prostitution. One informant, Nadia, a university student who had undergone sex reassignment surgery at the age of twenty, reported having sex with *farang* men for money on an occasional basis, although this was not her sole source of income. Here is an extract from the interview (carried out in English):

AB:　*So, tell me Nadia, do you sometimes have sex with men for money?*

N:　*[laughing] Yes!! But it is good to do like that — have a nice man — very nice! — because it is a very good job I think, have handsome man, and have money!!! [laughing] I never find any place a job like that!*

Indeed, Nadia then went on to report that this 'very good job' had enabled her to save up for her breast augmentation surgery. Nadia reported another occasion when she had met a naïve prospective client in a bar and had gone with him to a hotel room. On discovering that Nadia had a penis, the client had become so angry that Nadia was fearful that violence might ensue. However, the client calmed down and Nadia fell asleep. She awoke in the morning to find the client gone having left an envelope containing a large sum of money and a note saying, words to the effect, 'this money is for you, for your life'. Nadia saw this as a sign that the Buddha wanted her to have sex reassignment surgery and promptly phoned a surgeon with a view to having the operation at the earliest possible opportunity. Nadia underwent sex reassignment surgery the following week. Her perilously speedy transition was distinctly contrasting to that of transsexual women in England who commence their 'treatment' on the NHS, and find themselves involved in a protracted programme.

In Chiang Mai, another *kathoey*, a university graduate who is not a prostitute but who runs her own tourism business raised funds for sex reassignment surgery with money from her earnings, despite having to send money home to her parents who live in an impoverished rural village in Northern Thailand, and whose economic status is relatively poor. However, her story was not typical, in that many *kathoey* of this study, from similar backgrounds, who had undergone full sex-reassignment, had raised the funds through prostitution.

CHAPTER NINE
Trans-sexualities

It seems to me that *kathoey* are more 'sexually' motivated than the British transwomen of my study, who generally seemed more concerned with successfully living in the female role than having sex with men. However, the sexual preferences of transsexual people (as is the case in the general population) are characterised by diversity; sexual orientation covers heterosexual, homosexual, pansexual, bisexual and asexual. However, as I have argued elsewhere in this book, researchers in the past have categorized all *kathoey* as self-identifying as heterosexual women. Indeed, in my own research, asking *kathoey* in all categories about their sexual orientation (*'Khun yahg mee fairn poo-ying reu poo-chai na ka?'* [Translation: 'do you like to have a girlfriend or a boyfriend?']), brought forth the almost unanimous response, *'Poo-chai!! Poo-chai!!'* (Translation: 'Men! Men!'); many *kathoey* were incredulous at the suggestion that they could possibly be sexually attracted to anyone but men. One *kathoey* responded to my asking if she had ever been attracted to a woman, with *'Never in my mind!!'* and other *kathoey* reported that their boyfriends happily accepted them as women; while others reported that the important thing for them was that the partner was kind and had a 'good heart' (*jai dee*). However, this is only a small part of the picture as a whole. In fact, *kathoey* working in the sex industry or, indeed, those working as cabaret dancers, regularly have sex with each other.[41] *Kathoey* sexualities represent eclectic definitions; for example, as discussed earlier in this book, one group of *kathoey* 'market' themselves as *Sao Siabp*, or 'penetrating girls' in order to enhance their employment prospects in the sex industry. However, this should not be viewed as the whole picture but only one aspect of these *kathoeys'* sexualities. Some *kathoey* undergo sex reassignment surgery specifically to enhance their employment prospects. Others reported that they had

---

41 It is noteworthy that, as stated earlier in this book, I was myself, on two separate occasions, sexually propositioned by *kathoey* in bars; however, the author accepts that *kathoey* may well have been confused by the presence of a *farang* woman in a Ladyboy bar.

undergone sex reassignment surgery to please their boyfriends. We need to examine *kathoey* lives within the context of the broader sociological and anthropological picture of Thai culture and society.

British transsexual women's sexual orientation was equally diverse. Indeed, one British transsexual woman, in answer to my question as to her sexual orientation, boldly claimed, *'Anything with a pulse!'* Some of the British transsexual women of this study reported being 'attracted to *people*' rather than a particular gender, indicating, perhaps, a potential pan-sexual orientation. It is also the case that a pre-transitional transsexual whose sexual orientation was normatively heterosexual (in that they were attracted to women) may become heterosexual (attracted to men) post-operatively. A transwoman, then, who may have been an apparent heterosexual man pre-operatively, may, after transition become a heterosexual woman. Hence one transwoman vehemently denied any homosexual feelings prior to her transition, but recounted the occasion when, post-operatively, she found herself one day observing an attractive man for whom she experienced sexual desire. I know of at least one case of a post-operative male-to-female transsexual, who, having been a married man with children, went on to marry a genetic male partner. As at the time UK law did not provide for what would have been classed as a 'same-sex marriage', the couple, both British, married in Scandinavia[42]. Other transwomen formed lesbian relationships with either other transwomen or lesbian genetic women. As one professional interviewee explained to me,

> But most of them don't actually end up with a man ... I mean, many of them live with another woman ... and they suggest that they are lesbians and that is the way they want to be ...

In other cases, the male-to-female transsexual who may have been married and lived in the 'normative' heterosexual male role wishes, post-

---

42 With the enactment of the Gender Recognition Act, 2004, the law now recognises transsexual people in their new gender and makes provision for post-op transsexuals to marry in their new gender.

operatively, to retain the marriage, including sexual relations. However, this has caused problems within marriage, where the wife self-identifies as a heterosexual woman, and has no desire for a lesbian relationship.

Some transsexual women reported that they were celibate. One confessed to being sexually naïve (she was a virgin) but was also one of those who reported being 'attracted to people', which I took to be a non-committal response meaning that they were likely to find both men and women attractive, and whichever gender showed an interest in them, would be the person with whom they were most likely to enter into a relationship. The gender did not matter so much; it was the chance of a relationship that took priority.

Perhaps the most fascinating narrative of pre- and post-operative sexualities came from Kate, a former officer in the Royal Air Force. As a 'male' in the RAF and spending long periods of time away from home, Kate confessed to having had plenty of potential sexual opportunities with other women. However, she stated that pre-transition, her wife was the only woman (indeed the only person) with whom she had had a sexual relationship. Kate spoke frankly about her sexuality and the effects that a current relationship with a male partner was having upon her. She reported,

Kate: *I always got on very well with women ... many women made it plain to me that they would have liked to have gone to bed with me ... but I behaved myself impeccably when I was away ...*

AB: *Yes, I am sure, I can well imagine. And so it was there for you, on a plate, and you never did anything about it?*

K: *Mm. But I still can't explain it and I still can't exclude the possibility that there may be some aspect to my sexuality that I have not discovered yet ... but the only experimentation that I have done [post transition] has been with men. There have been two unsuccessful attempts and one ongoing highly successful, which I find extremely good. And you know, it makes me feel wanted, it makes me feel desirable, it makes me feel very good and it makes me feel very satisfied ... and you know, that's very good I think.*

During previous interviews I carried out with transsexual women, it seemed to me that the final confirmation of their 'femininity' came from their post-operative sexual experiences with men, a notion that had sat uncomfortably with my feminist Self. I wondered if Kate's experience reported above had produced the same effect. I asked her,

AB: *Does it feel at all like an affirmation of your femininity?*

K: *I worry about that, because I have often thought about many people in my situation who have thought to themselves, 'I have got to go to bed with a man because unless I have had sex with a man I am not a woman at all'. In other words, 'unless I am a woman in a man's eyes, I am not a woman at all', and I would never subscribe to that.*

AB: *No, no. And no feminist would, either.*

K: *Exactly! Absolutely! I mean, I am perfectly competent myself as a woman without the intervention of any man. It doesn't alter the fact that this third experience, well, it is not an affirmation of myself at all, that's not it at all; it has made me feel good about myself in a way that I never have. I mean, I have always had terribly low self-esteem.*

AB: *Really? [I am palpably shocked; Kate comes across as a very confident, competent and self-reliant person]*

K: *Yes, I have. Absolutely ... and suddenly, this man, there he was telling me that I was gorgeous, that I was good in bed ... and my self-esteem went whizzing up!*

I ventured to ask Kate if her experience with this man had perhaps had the effect of affirming her as a desirable woman.

K: *Desirable, yes. I think the word is desirable. I think you are absolutely right. And you know, somebody else _wanted_ me ... so I am having a lot of fun making love as a heterosexual woman.*

For Kate, then, affirmation of her desirability as a woman came from her successful relationship with the new man in her life. For transsexual women the importance of being as 'perfect' and 'authentic' a woman as possible can lead to fears of not being 'good enough' as a woman. For some, this means 'passing' as a 'perfect' or 'authentic' woman. However, although vaginal intercourse serves to help some transwomen to pass their 'final examination' and graduate into 'womanhood', ultimate womanhood eludes them: they cannot give birth. In some sense, then, transsexual women and *kathoey* are 'artificial' women, in that they can only approximate a change of sex. They 'imitate' 'natural' women in many ways, except in the realms of woman's single power: childbirth. Hence, they remain, Virtual Women.

As noted elsewhere (Billings and Urban, 1982), transwomen can be at risk of becoming 'polysurgical' in their quest for the perfect female body image. For some, it would seem, sexual perfection is a goal in itself. I would like to share with you Marion's story, a transsexual woman whose quest for 'perfect' womanhood produced pre-operative anxieties regarding outcome.

'Sexual *Jouissance*': The Illusory transsexual dream

It seems to me that, for many transsexual women, 'perfect' womanhood equates to aspirations of what Jacque Lacan calls '*jouissance*': an illusive dream that is virtually unattainable. The question is, can *jouissance* for the transwoman, ever be achieved? Orgasm during coitus manifests as a '*petit mort*', or 'little death'. For some newly reborn 'heterosexual' transwomen, sexual *jouissance* can only be achieved via vaginal penetrative intercourse with a man, who serves to 'confirm' or at least 'affirm' their state of womanhood. However, the desire for sexual *jouissance* and the ambitious desire for the achievement of *jouissance*, is illusory; it depends for its realization not only on post-operative sexual relations with a man, but the '*petit mort*' of the old Self and the birth (or rebirth) of the body in the female form, that as closely as possible resembles that of the genetic woman. For some, the desire for *jouissance* is so intense, that the thwarting of its achievement can mean the replacement of its desire by a desire for death. Yet *jouissance*, for the transsexual being, is never quite enough; it can be achieved yet at the same time not achieved, as it necessarily entails a compromise. As Marion explained to me on the eve of leaving for Thailand for her sex reassignment surgery:

> *...if something happened and I couldn't fix it, I don't know what I would do, because I am not an 'in-betweenie', ... well, I don't know what I would do, it would be very serious, I think I would be back down that road and considering ending it [committing suicide]. And it is so important, I can't explain it ... I want to make love as a woman and be penetrated and all of those things ... It is an essential part of being, for me. For some people ... it is OK, but for me, no, ... I realise I cannot be a woman in the same way as a real girl, you know ... But, I have to be the best I can possibly be. And my big, big, big fear is that, even if I am the best I can possibly be, it won't be enough.*

Marion's story suggests that she prefers death to thwarted *jouissance*. For the transsexual woman, the achievement of *jouissance* involves the *petit mort* of transition by the shedding of the unwanted (male) Self as a means to the rebirth of the new 'Other'. As Marion's account indicates, the denial or insufficiency of 'being the best I can possibly be' means the total death of both the physical and psychical self.

CHAPTER TEN

Social Acceptance
Transgender and its Social and Legal Incompatibilities

*The central feature of the stigmatized individual's
situation in life can now be stated. It is a question of
what is often, if vaguely, called 'acceptance'.
(Goffman, 1963, p.19)*

Let us now undertake a comparative examination of the different levels of social acceptance, non-acceptance and stigma experienced by transsexuals in England and *kathoey* in Thailand. I'd like to explore gender identity politics and show how, historically, transsexual individuals in England have been trapped 'betwixt and between' when it comes to their legal status. The attempts of political activists to redress this issue are also discussed here. I look at some of the legal issues concerning transsexual people, including marriage, birth certificates, parenthood, and employment and at the ways that the Gender Recognition Act 2004 (GRA) has addressed some of these issues, yet still falls short of affording equal opportunities to transsexual people in the United Kingdom. I also examine the *kathoey's* anomalous status when it comes to Thai law and illustrate the ways in which Thai law impacts upon the personal and public lives of *kathoey*.

Goffman's (1963) ideas concerning social acceptance are articulated in what he says about spoilt identity, stigma and acceptance. In his book, *The Presentation of Self in Everyday Life*, Goffman (1959) presents society as a theatre, with individual members of society as actors, 'dramaturgically' performing the 'script' of life. 'Playing the role' enables us to understand another's perspective and to see how our actions affect other 'actors' as we interact with them. Human society, then, is a stage upon which people 'perform' the 'script of life'. However, as with any theatrical performance, it is sometimes the case that the individual or 'actor' finds it necessary to improvise in order to keep the 'play' or performance going for the audience or, indeed, the world or society at large. For the transsexual person, learning to improvise and fit into a bipolar gendered society is crucial; without the skills involved in improvisation, the transsexual person is exposed as the actor who forgot her or his lines. This can result in what Goffman calls a 'spoilt identity' and social stigma inevitably ensues. In Thailand, many *kathoey* perform their transgender status on a real stage for a public audience. Some aspire to enter the *kathoey* beauty pageants that take place all over Thailand, but perhaps the two most spectacular of which take place in Pattaya. (I return to the *kathoey* beauty contest later in this chapter.) *Kathoey* also perform their 'female' selves in the public domain — the street — as well as on stage. Personal appearance is central to the *kathoey's* sense of self-identity. Even to those who do not perform their transgender status for a paying audience, personal appearance and the management of a 'spoilt' identity is of utmost importance. (Later in this chapter I consider the narrative of Wan, which illustrates this point). Observing *kathoey* in public places such as the shopping mall, the beauty salon, or some other every-day situation, one is subjected to the *kathoey* as 'court jester'. The role she plays serves to amuse the general public, her gender performance a parody of a woman. Thus, she 'manages' her cross-gender status to the point of social acceptance, over-compensating for a 'spoilt' identity. Another kind of *kathoey* 'performance' is sexual performance. Recall those *kathoey* I categorize as 'true Ladyboys' proudly claimed they could 'do anything' sexually that a woman can do, *and more'*. Sexual performance, then, formed an integral part of their self-identity as *kathoey*.

'Managing' the transgender experience

As stated elsewhere in this work, transsexual people find ways of 'managing' their stigmatized existence. The *kathoey* does this in a variety of ways: by taking on the role of court jester, by 'performing' their transgender status in highly sophisticated cabaret shows, and by exhibition in elaborate, spectacular beauty pageants. In England, transsexual and transgender people have found ways of managing their lives through what Goffman calls a 'virtual identity' rather than in their 'actual identity'. They 'pretend' to be that (unwanted) gender which, by societal mores they are bound to accept because by social or legal prohibition, their 'actual identity' is illegitimate. Stephen Whittle states:

The real world has medically, socially and legally failed to afford a place in which they can authenticate themselves (2002, p.83) [emphasis mine].

The post-op transsexual person strives at perfecting her or himself as a 'passing' female or male, or some notion of feminine or masculine 'realness' (Whittle, 2002, p.87). For some, an assimilationist approach is a completely unviable proposition, because they will never 'pass'. For others, 'passing' means total non-disclosure of their transsexual status and thus every new relationship, whether with friends, potential partners or employers, begins with a lie (or an 'untruth' or at least an economy of the 'truth', having lied by omission). Changing the law to allow transsexuals to marry in their 'new' gender does not of course automatically assume that marriage is attainable. Some transsexual women, keenly aware of this, I discovered, will keep their transgender status from a new partner, only to be disappointed when he discovers her 'secret' and terminates the relationship. But surely the onus is not on the trans partner to 'pass' as a woman. Such relationships, if they are to be successful, are also contingent upon acceptance and tolerance on the part of potential partners. As long as such 'deceit' goes on with new relationships, the more disappointment will ensue, for those transsexual people who deceive in order to 'pass', deny themselves the opportunity of genuine relationships. However, the legal right to private life should assume to espouse the right to keep private a person's personal history of transsexual status, but only if this does not harm or deceive others whom, like potential spouses, one could argue, have a moral right to know. Nonetheless, one could also argue that the ability or inability to 'pass' or not should be immaterial when it comes to the right to personal and physical safety, equal employment or other opportunities, or indeed full legal equality. At the same time, a legal ban on discrimination against transsexuals, whether in respect of employment or any other aspect of life, does not guarantee protection against discrimination or intolerance either in the workplace or anywhere else in the social sphere. In Britain, there is legal recourse under the terms of the Sex Discrimination (Gender Reassignment) Act, 1999 and the Gender Recognition Act (2004), which allows for the transsexual victim to claim compensation on the grounds of such discrimination, and to be legally recognised in their new gender. Under Thai law, the *kathoey* enjoys no such legal protection. She is legally classified and treated as male all of her life. The *kathoey* is not allowed to legally change her male name to a female name, and her personal documents remain in her male name for all of her life.

Transgender and UK Law: The Gender Recognition Act, 2004

Hi Anne! Great news! Have got my GRC!
Can now get married!
All I have to do is find a victim –
Whoops, sorry! I mean a husband!
(Text message sent to the author from a transwoman in UK, Jan, 2006).

The new Gender Recognition Act (2004) — known as the GRA — came into force in April 2005 and serves to address the discrimination that transsexuals have been subjected to in the past and offers legal recognition to transsexuals, giving them access to the same rights as those afforded to other people born into the same gender. Transsexual women, then, are now legally recognised as women, and transsexual men are legally recognised as men.

The Gender Identity Research and Education Society (GIRES) and transgender political activist group, *Press for Change* worked towards a Gender Recognition Act that would serve to protect the rights of couples' marriages that had taken place before one of the partners had transitioned. It serves as well to allow marriage to take place between couples where one partner is transsexual, meaning that both parties are the same 'birth' or 'biological' sex. Couples who were married before the transition of one partner were required to divorce before the GRA came into force.

The passing of the GRA means that transsexuals can apply to the 'Gender Recognition Panel' to be issued with a 'Gender Recognition Certificate' (GRC). As aforementioned, under UK law, until the enactment of the GRA, transsexuals were not legally recognised in their 'new' or 'acquired' gender for certain purposes, such as marriage. Applications can now be made to the Gender Recognition Panel by transsexuals aged over 18, who (1) suffer with gender dysphoria, (2) have been living in the acquired gender for a minimum of two years, and (3) intend to carry on living in that gender. Evidence of transgender status is required in the form of reports from two doctors, of which one must be working in the field of gender dysphoria, or a report from a chartered psychologist and one other registered medical practitioner. It is a requirement that medical reports include details of diagnosis of 'gender dysphoria'. The applicant must have undergone sex reassignment treatment or been prescribed such treatment or planning to undergo treatment to change the sexual characteristics of their body to match the acquired gender. This generated anxiety amongst transsexual people who had made application to the Gender Recognition Panel for issue of a Gender Recognition Certificate, and had been asked by the Panel for further clarification as to the extent of the 'treatment' they had undergone. The fear was that if they had not undergone genital altering surgery, they might not be classed as being 'transsexual' or of having transitioned. Christine Burns of pfc posted assurances that this was not the case and the Panel was on the 'side' of transsexuals and not out to deny them their legal right to a GRC.

A statutory declaration as to whether the applicant is married or not is required, and if not married, provided all conditions have been satisfied, a full GRC is issued. However, if the applicant is still married, an interim GRC will be issued until the marriage has been dissolved. There is a right of appeal to the High Court against rejected applications, and if the appeal is also rejected, then the transperson has to wait six months before making another application for a GRC. The issuing of a Gender Recognition Certificate means that thereafter for all purposes, the transperson is classified as belonging to the acquired gender, for example, a transsexual man ('transman') becomes a 'man' and a transsexual woman ('transwoman') becomes a 'woman' under UK law. The Secretary of State sends a copy of the GRC to the Registrar General, who keeps a copy of the original Birth Certificate or Adoption Certificate. Parental status is not affected by the issuing of a GRC, so a female-to-male transsexual retains the status of 'mother' of 'her' children, and a male-to-female transsexual retains the status of 'father' to 'his' children. Matters of 'property', 'succession' and 'peerage' remain unaffected by the issue of a Gender Recognition Certificate.

However, in some senses the Gender Recognition Act 2004 could be viewed as not always serving transsexual people well. Transpeople are eligible to marry in their new gender, once they have received the Gender Recognition Certificate. Pre-existing marriages, where one partner has transitioned to the same gender as their spouse, are not required to divorce. However, transsexuals and their spouses still faced an unresolved situation, as the partners in such a marriage will either be required to divorce once the GRC has been issued, or, alternatively, if the couple wish to stay married then there can be no issuing of the GRC. This requirement causes distress to couples whose marriage has survived the transition of one partner, and who wish to remain married. Loyal wives of long-lasting marriages to male-to-female transsexuals suffer financial loss, as they are denied pension and other benefits to which they would be entitled based on a husband's national insurance contributions or private pension plan. The alternative is for the transsexual partner of the marriage to forego the right to a Gender Recognition Certificate.[43]

Other areas of legal anomaly exist in Britain. The GRA is also viewed by some transfolk as unfair in other areas of everyday life. For example, gender-specific sport precludes competitors from taking part in competitive sports in their acquired gender. Therefore, a male-to-female transsexual cannot compete in a women's hockey team or play tennis as a competitive sport in her acquired gender, as this could be regarded as giving her an unfair advantage over genetic women opponents whose average physical size and strength are less than those of a 'male' competitor. However, male-to-female transsexuals lose a lot of 'masculine' strength due to taking female hormones, and this is one reason why some transsexual people view such legislation as unfavourable. An example of favourable legislation, however, occurs under criminal law. Gender-specific criminal offences apply to the transsexual person's acquired gender. For example, under the Sexual Offences Act, 2004, a male-to-

43 I am grateful to Mrs Terry Reed, JP, (GIRES) for her kind help in clarifying these points for me.

female transsexual person can be recognised as a victim of rape, a law that serves to accept that transsexual women may be vulnerable and in need of protection just as is the case for 'biological' women. By the same token, however, a female-to-male transsexual can, hypothetically, be charged with rape, although the likelihood of such an occurrence diminishes somewhat in light of the fact that many transmen have not undergone or indeed choose not to undergo phalloplasty, as the surgical technique for the fashioning of a fully functioning penis is as yet relatively unsophisticated.

Finally, UK law now protects the privacy of transsexual persons. The GRA states that it is an offence for a person who has acquired 'protected information' in an official capacity to disclose the information to any other person. The new legislation that results from the GRA brings the rest of UK law into line with the Sex Discrimination Act (Gender Reassignment) Act 1999, which affords protection against discrimination to transsexuals in terms of employment and vocational training and to be treated as unequivocally belonging to their new acquired gender.

Gender Identity Politics — claiming a legal status

Previous to the Gender Recognition Act, however, transsexual people in Britain have existed in a legal limbo-land. Justice has been denied to transsexual people in Britain on the grounds of taboo, prejudice and intolerance, and through a lack of understanding of the 'medical' condition that is called 'gender dysphoria' or a lack of understanding of 'transsexualism'. This has led to decision-makers, corporate managers and government giving trans-related issues low priority as they found perhaps less controversial and more 'urgent' issues to deal with. This could also be due to the relative rarity of the transgender phenomenon within the context of the general population. Hence trans-gender has not been legitimised or recognised. Consequently, in the past, 'gender migrants' in Britain have found themselves still 'betwixt and between' when it comes to the law, and this impacts on issues of employment, insurance, prison placement, marriage and the family. Thus, transsexuals in Britain have faced legal discrimination. Even though it has been legal for transsexuals to change their names on personal and official documents, when it comes to recognition of their new gender, until very recently, UK law had failed them. Hence while it has been possible to amend driver's licences, bank details, passports and other such documents to take into account the new 'female' or 'male' names, transsexual people could neither acquire an amended birth certificate nor to marry in their acquired gender. Consequently, while any mentally competent adult in the UK can undergo hormone treatment, sex reassignment surgery and related surgeries to effect a physical change of gender, such a person remained, thereafter, obliged to live their lives 'betwixt and between' in gender. Over time it became clear to legislators what had been clear to transsexuals, and their families, partners and 'significant others' for years: that new legislation was needed that would redress the inequalities that existed and which denied to the transsexual person in UK, equal opportunities and legal and human rights.

For decades, transsexual political activists in Britain have been campaigning to claim legal status that affords them some legitimacy. Transsexual activists have sought a 'unique set of freedoms' (Whittle, 1998) that the law would acknowledge, giving them the same rights as other women and men. That later translated into a different 'set of freedoms': to be legally recognised specifically as 'transwomen' and 'transmen'. Such status as transwomen/men rejects the bipolar model of gender, and replaces it with a tripartite model, not dissimilar to the female/male/third gender paradigm that exists in other cultures such as Thailand. However, Sandy Stone, in her work titled *The Empire Strikes Back* ... (1991), rejects a 'third gender' as problematic and instead espouses 'a *genre* — a set of embodied texts' with the potential to disrupt 'structured sexualities' (Stone, 1991, p.296, emphasis in original). Moreover, as transman Stephen Whittle argues, a 'third gender' category for transsexuals is not what transgender political activists seek to espouse. Instead, transsexuals have moved from claiming their rights from within the existing binary poles of gender, to claiming the need to express their gender whilst accepting the existence of gender roles as articulated from within the male-female dichotomous model. Article 8 of the European Convention on Human Rights states that, *'Everyone has the right to respect for his* [sic] *private and family life, his* [sic] *home and his* [sic] *correspondence ...'* (EConHR, cited in Whittle, 1998). In the past, transsexuals have been denied equality and respect for their private and family lives (Whittle, 2002). Let us now examine some of these inequalities.

Marriage

In Britain forty years ago (1971), the marriage of post-op male-to-female transsexual April Ashley and Arthur Corbett (*Corbett-v-Corbett*) was ruled to be null and void by the judge, Mr Justice Ormrod, on the ground that Ashley's birth sex was male, and therefore a marriage between two males could not be deemed lawful (Whittle, 2002, pp.8-9). This case then set a precedent and thereafter no two people with the same chromosomes were allowed to marry in the UK.[44] While Corbett had married Ashley in the full knowledge of her transsexual status, he claimed that the marriage had not been consummated. The ruling that the marriage was judged null and void and unconsummated meant that Ashley was not entitled to any financial settlement that divorce would have brought her. So that let Corbett off the hook! In the years that followed, transsexuals were to robustly campaign for the right to private life, the right to marry in their 'new' gender and to receive state pension (in the case of the male-to-female at the age of sixty), as has normally been the case for 'genetic' women.

The gendered birth certificate and its effects for transsexuals

Another area of legal discrimination of transsexuals has been the issue of birth certificates. Stephen Whittle, a law academic and vice-president of the transgender and transsexual political activist group, *Press for Change*, championed campaigns by transsexuals in Britain to have their birth certificates changed to their 'new' gender and to be recognised as such under UK law. British transsexuals have taken litigious

---

44 Some 'lesbian' couples have used this law to their advantage. In 1998, transsexual woman Tracy O'Keefe married her biological woman lesbian partner in a registry office in London. However, this marriage was delayed for some months as the Superintendent Registrar mistook O'Keefe for a 'biological' woman, and refused to perform the marriage ceremony (O'Keefe, 1999:292-298; personal communication, O'Keefe, 2000).

action against the UK Government claiming a breach of Article 8 of the European Convention on Human Rights (EConHR), because they have been unable to change their birth certificates to reflect their new gender, and therefore have been denied the right to marry in their new gender. In 1986, female-to-male transsexual Mark Rees lost his legal action against the UK Government in the European Court of Human Rights (ECHR) when the Court held by a majority of 12–3 votes, that amendment of the birth certificate would in effect be re-writing history, based on the premise that a birth certificate is a document with historical status and serves to record an event that has in fact occurred. In such a case, the 'current civil status' (Whittle, 1998) of Rees as a transman would override an historical event, that is, Rees was apparently female when he was born. Similarly, in 1990, Caroline Cossey, a British transsexual woman, lost her legal battle to allow her to marry a man, when the ECHR by a majority of 10 votes to 8, held that to have her birth certificate amended to enable her to marry did not contravene Article 8 of the Convention, in that it did not constitute a breach of her right to private life (Whittle, 1998).

More cases were lost, as were subsequent appeals, before being taken further to the ECHR in Strasbourg. A breakthrough finally occurred in 2002, when transwoman, Christine Goodwin, and another anonymous transsexual woman were successful in taking their independent cases to the ECHR having had them rejected under UK law. Goodwin's case asked for (1) the UK Government to award her a state pension at the age of sixty, rather than at sixty-five, in accordance with the right of 'biological' women so to do; (2) the UK Government to issue her with a new National Insurance number, and (3) to allow her to marry her male partner. The UK Government's failure to alter birth certificates of transsexual people and to allow them to marry in their new gender was held by the ECHR to be in breach of the European Convention on Human Rights (*Goodwin-v-United Kingdom* and *"I"-v-United Kingdom* (2002) [35 EUR R18] (cited by *Press for Change*). Goodwin's case was a landmark victory, which eventually led to a change in British law, and *Press for Change* activists urged other transsexuals to claim their rights following the ECHR Court victory. This meant that, under international law, the UK was obliged to change its laws that discriminated against transsexual people. The ruling also effectively forced the British government to change the law to allow an amendment of the birth certificate of transsexual people to reflect their 'new' gender and to be able to marry as such and receive the state pension at the age of sixty for transsexual women and sixty-five for transsexual men.

The European Court of Human Rights recognised that for transsexuals to effect a change of gender involved many painful and irreversible surgical procedures, and that these could be carried out under the supervision of the NHS, that itself acknowledged the existence of the 'medical condition' called 'gender dysphoria' or 'transsexualism' and provided treatment. The Court also argued that any medical discourse on the aetiology of transsexualism held no real significance, or legal relevance with regard to human rights issues, and that it was no longer sustainable that transsexuals should exist in a legal limbo-land that had no designated gender status for them (Press for Change, undated). It then followed that transsexuals should be allowed to marry a person of the 'opposite' gender (of that transsexual person's acquired gender); thus a transsexual woman can marry a 'biological' man. Hence the judgment of Judge Ormrod in the Corbett v. Corbett case no longer holds for transsexual people today, and infertility (as is the case for a post-op transsexual person) will not lead to an annulment of a marriage where one partner (or both for that matter) is transsexual.

A further case in 1997 involved an application to the Court by a transman, named as 'X' and his female partner 'Y', for permission to have 'X' registered as the father of 'Y's birth child, 'Z', who had been conceived by artificial insemination by donor. The request was refused on the ground that only a 'biological' man could be registered as the father of a child so conceived. It seems to me that, in effect, this meant that UK law at that time deemed a person born with *biologically* female genitalia to be incapable of successfully fulfilling the *social* role of 'father' to his children. In such a case, biology takes precedence over social status. The case was taken to the ECHR (*X, Y & Z v. UK Government*, 1997, cited by *Press for Change*, undated) the plaintiffs invoking Article 8, '... the right to respect for private and family life ...'. The ECHR ruled that while the UK Government had breached Article 8, the Court also recognised that there being no common standard in Europe when it comes to parental rights for transsexual individuals, Article 8 does not, or rather, cannot apply, as to do so would imply that the UK Government was obliged to recognise a person who is not a 'biological' male as the father of a child (Whittle, 1998). Another area of discrimination against transsexuals in Britain has been in the area of employment. I will now examine some cases of discrimination in the workplace.

Employment

A number of the transsexual women taking part in my research reported having taken legal action against former or prospective employers, on the grounds of discrimination in the workplace, and subsequently awarded damages. By way of example, I will discuss the case of 'Susan'. Susan's case has been freely available for anyone to read on the Internet; however, she also recounted the case to me during the course of an interview. The following account is taken from that interview.

In the days before the GRA (2004) and the earlier Sex Discrimination (Gender Reassignment) Act, 1999 came into force there was no recourse for transsexuals who had faced discrimination in the workplace. Susan started life as a male and was a qualified barrister who had enjoyed a highly successful career spanning twenty-three years, in the Royal Navy. In 1988, Susan, then still 'male', decided to leave the Navy. In 1992 he applied and was accepted for the post of Crown Prosecutor at the Crown Prosecution Service (CPS), and, having finally decided to transition from male to female, and start her new job as 'Susan', wrote to the Director of Public Prosecutions, explaining the situation. In light of the disclosure, the offer of employment was withdrawn. Despite Susan's remonstrations, Mills reiterated that the decision was final. For Susan, the situation emphasised the great difficulties involved in applying for a job as a man, while wanting to work as a woman. Her qualifications, although impeccable, were all registered in her previous male identity. Susan felt that she had no option but to accept the final decision of the DPP.

However, in 1996, the ECJ in Luxembourg, which interprets the law retrospectively, ruled that European Equal treatment laws protect transsexuals from discrimination in employment. Although Susan's case, by this time some time past, was 'out of time', under the terms of the ECJ ruling she could now bring her case against the CPS once more. The CPS, having lost the case at an industrial tribunal, appealed, but lost. On the day that a further appeal by the CPS was due to start, the CPS finally conceded that Susan's transsexual status should not have inhibited her employment prospects with the Service and settled the matter out of court with an undisclosed sum of compensation. As a result of the case, the Crown Prosecution Service put in place appropriate equal opportunities policies to ensure that such discrimination could not occur within the Service again (interview by the author with Susan, 2001).

The Precarious relationship between the Transsexual woman and Criminal Law

For the transsexual person who does not 'pass', there exists a need to be watchful and alert to possible danger whenever she or he is out in public. At any time, the transsexual person who is 'read' in public can, hypothetically, run the risk of criminal proceedings being taken against them. In certain circumstances, the transsexual/transgender person in a public place is in danger of being arrested and charged with 'conduct likely to cause a breach of the peace'. However, precisely what 'conduct' might be construed as 'likely to cause a breach of the peace' is somewhat difficult to ascertain.

A preliminary investigation carried out to determine just what 'conduct' by a transsexual person might be likely to cause a breach of the peace obtained very limited results. Indeed, the only example of a transsexual woman who might be involved in 'conduct likely to cause a breach of the peace' that emerged was the transsexual woman dressed in feminine attire and using a female public toilet. As Whittle (2002, p.115) states, there seems to exist in Britain, a 'national neurosis' about toilets when it comes to the gender division of 'male' and 'female' public facilities. Hypothetically, if a woman in a public toilet confronted by a transsexual woman was to scream, although the scream had emitted from the woman, responsibility for 'causing' that scream fell upon the transsexual woman. Consequently, should the police be called to investigate, the transsexual woman could quite legitimately be arrested and charged (Whittle e-mail communication, February, 2005; Norfolk Constabulary, personal communication, February, 2005). A visit of enquiry to my local police station in Norwich brought forth no other examples of possibilities as to what kind of 'conduct' might be construed as 'likely to cause a breach of the peace'. It seems we are limited to the toilet scenario. My grateful thanks are due to Stephen Whittle (e-mail communication, 2005) and to the two Police Constables of Norfolk Constabulary, "Steve" and "Dave", who kindly explained the law in this regard, and then phoned the Crown Prosecution Service to enquire as to whether any transsexual woman had ever been charged with this offence or any other 'conduct likely to cause a breach of the peace' in Norwich. There had been one previous case, and the accused was found not guilty. Apart from this the records revealed that, as far as transsexuals are concerned no such charge of 'conduct likely ...' has ever been brought to court in Norwich (February 2005). Stephen Whittle also confirmed that no such case had been brought against any transsexual person in Britain in the past twenty years.

It seems to me a curious situation that, while in Britain it is within the law to undergo gender reassignment, that same law then denies civil and human rights to the fully transitioned transsexual woman or man, to the extent that a perfectly innocent transsexual woman faces the risk of police action for an 'imaginary' offence (in a public toilet) that she has not committed.

I have highlighted here just some anomalies of law that transsexual people have faced in the past and how some of these anomalies can now be addressed in light of the Gender Recognition Act (2004), as well as the shortcomings of the Act. While the Sex Discrimination (Gender Reassignment) Act 1999 and the Gender Recognition Act 2004 go some way towards remedying legal inconsistencies, these do not address the issues of the *social* attitudes to transsexual people and their significant others. So, let us now examine social acceptance and non-acceptance as experienced by some of the transwomen of my research.

Social Acceptance — Britain

The mental, emotional and physical wellbeing of transsexual people is affected by their experiences of the social stigma that often accompanies this condition, and this, somewhat unsurprisingly, has significant implications which impact on their social and personal lives. In England, a change of sex has been in the past, and is still today, a *cause célèbre* and the transsexual person viewed as 'fair game' for the sensationalist stories published by the tabloid press designed to feed the public appetite for spicy gossip. Despite legislation by the Government to change the law, tabloids will grasp the opportunity to publish transsexual people's stories in lurid terms. This often means that, although the law in England and, indeed, the rest of the UK, supposedly 'protects' the human rights of the individual, the transsexual person who cannot 'pass' convincingly can face, at best ridicule, at worst verbal and/or physical abuse at street level. Sally is a British transsexual woman that I met in Thailand. After having undergone sex reassignment surgery, Sally was approached by a magazine with a request to publish her story. According to her account, after agreeing to this and posing for photographs, the magazine then contacted Sally and asked permission to sell the story to a tabloid newspaper, with the promise that she would be well paid by the newspaper concerned. Sally reported that the magazine never published her story, but that three tabloids published it in grossly sensationalist terms that distorted and embellished Sally's account of her transition. Tellingly, in somewhat offensive terms, one tabloid report refers to Sally in the male pronoun throughout, thereby displaying blatant disregard and disrespect. Sally told me that she has never received payment from any of these tabloids.

The stories of the participants of my research suggest that the transsexual person in the West suffers verbal, physical and emotional abuse, entirely due to their transgender status. The majority of the transsexuals from England that I interviewed reported having come up against non-acceptance, even hostility from close family members. Let us take a look at some of these now ...

Transsexual women and their families: acceptance and non-acceptance

Let us now look at the stories of some transsexual people who have experienced both acceptance and non-acceptance by their families. What follows are stories, which highlight some typical experiences of being a transgendered person. I begin with an e-mail I received from a British transsexual woman in her sixties, who had read an article, published on the TransgenderASIA website I had written about Tinar, my *kathoey* friend in Chiang Mai:

Alison's story:

> *'Dear Anne,*
> *I read your article on "Tinar, Thailand"*[45] *just now on the TG Asia web site and was moved to congratulate you on the very moving account of this young lady and her own and her family's positive outlook on life. As I think you are aware, I had surgery in Thailand last year and have never felt better able to cope with life, despite my age. I do wish I could have had some support from my family but things were entirely different as I was married and had sired*[46] *two [children]. However, not all is lost there as we do talk and see each other from time to time. If only society had been more accepting in my younger days things would have been different and life more tolerable. But we can never have everything can we? So I do not regret having a family, which is something I will cherish to my dying day.'*

Susie's story:

Susie is thirty-seven years old and is currently in the middle of her transition from male to female. While Susie's close friends and employer

---

45 http://web.hku.hk/~sjwinter/TransgenderASIA/index.htm

46 This is an interesting use of language: by using the term 'sired' rather than 'fathered', Alison seems to be either denying or at least trying to distance herself from her previous male status as a father.

have accepted and supported her in her transition, her father and brother were, at first, not so accommodating. She told me:

> *I have got a brother. He knows but he don't really understand 'cause he came up to me and said, 'now, if you are changing sex', he said, 'what about if me and my girlfriend have a baby, what am I going to tell the child?' I said, 'it's easy, just say this is your Aunty Susie, you don't need to say anything else' ... My father thinks it's a cold and I am going to get better ... when I told him that I'd started hormones he said 'alright' and from then on I leave messages on the phone and I write to him but he don't want to know ...*

Although Susie's family did not accept her, the story was a different one when it came to telling her neighbours:

> S: *... That was the most worrying thing, actually telling my neighbours. That was like, 'Oh Dear! How am I going to tell them? Then I thought, sod it! I'll just go and tell them!'*
>
> AB: *So were you already friendly with them?*
>
> S: *Yes, I was friendly, but since I told them I know them better than I have ever done ... now we go out and have an evening meal. We go swimming every Tuesday. I know some of [the neighbour's] friends and they come swimming as well. They are all fascinated by it. I tell them all about it and that.*

Susie works as a nurse, caring for an elderly lady in her own home, going in to work on a daily basis. I asked her if she went to work dressed as 'Susie'. Here is what she had to say:

> S: *At the moment I tend to dress down a bit. Where she lives ... there is a lot of ignorant morons up there to put it bluntly, so I tend to dress down. Just to not attract any attention ... I don't care about myself but at the moment, until I look more feminine I try to tend to keep it fairly low key just for*

*her sake. I don't want any trouble for her. There are still a
lot of ignorant bigots out there who just have no clue.*

Lucy's story:

Lucy is now a fully transitioned transsexual woman in her thirties,
whose narrative highlights the need for the raising of awareness of the
transgender phenomenon. According to Lucy, she was wrongly convicted
for the crime of grievous bodily harm, and was in the middle of her
'real life experience' when she was given a custodial sentence and, as a
pre-op transsexual woman, incarcerated in a men's prison. Lucy recalled
the initiative taken by a fellow prisoner, who had set himself up as her
'protector' during her early days in prison:

Lucy: *This guy, he had been in prison for eleven years, a hard-nut
sort of type. He said — apparently — I heard from the nurses
that he'd been round -because they knew I was coming — they
get word — and when they knew I was coming there he went
round and told every prisoner, that if he heard that any of
them was giving me a hard time, they would have him to
deal with. That I was a woman and it was ridiculous what
they were doing. So he knew, but the officers ...*

AB: *So how did he get to know? And how was he so aware ...?*

L: *It is going to shock you! Paddington Green! [Docu-drama
on British television, which featured 'Jackie', a transsexual
woman who was working as a prostitute to fund her own
sex reassignment surgery] ... And I had never watched
Paddington Green but he had watched the programme and
he'd got an insight from that ... and that guy saved my life
for those months ... he looked after me ... it was almost as if
he had been put there to look after me ...*

The fear of possible physical or verbal abuse is a real concern for the
transsexual woman who does not easily 'pass'.

Angela's story:

I met Angela, a British post-op transsexual woman in Thailand, where she had undergone facial feminization surgery. She recalled a potentially violent incident in a pub:

> *Angela: ... this guy in his late twenties and he was quite drunk and he saw me from my profile and literally I am sitting there and he comes right up to me and says 'fuck me, it's a bloke'. I mean, quite honestly, that was just ignorance, but it could equally have been turned into something quite nasty. And that is one of the reasons why I have had facial surgery ... he obviously saw something that ... rang alarm bells in his mind and just had to come over and take a closer look ... it is frightening ...*

Mary's story:

Mary, a forty-four year old transsexual woman I also met in Thailand, sold her home in England in order to afford the cost of sex reassignment surgery, and had moved into a rented flat in a rough part of the city where she lives. As a transsexual person who does not easily 'pass', she was anxious about being 'read' by local people and the inevitable verbal and physical abuse that she felt was sure to follow. Mary worried that upon discovery, there would inevitably be 'bricks thrown through the window' as well as verbal harassment and physical violence. For this transsexual woman, then, the fear of harassment was never far away. Now let us look at the ways that some Western religious beliefs can impact on the lives of transsexual women.

Religion and acceptance

A woman must not dress like a man,
nor a man like a woman;
anyone who does this is detestable to YAHWEH your God.
(Deuteronomy 22:v.5)

The 'Christian Church' in Britain has traditionally been regarded as a sanctuary for the persecuted or pursued. Indeed, in the past, criminal fugitives have found shelter in the Church, protected from the law. However, the sanctuary of the Christian church does not always extend to transsexual persons. In 2001 evangelical Christians in Britain openly opposed transsexualism and argued for a veto of sex reassignment surgeries and admonishing transsexuals to 'pray to God' to make them 'normal'. Transsexualism, they argued, goes against 'God's will' (Southam, 2001). In 2000 and again in 2005, Anglican Bishops gave their approval for two transsexual Church ministers to transition from male to female and remain incumbents of the Church. However, Bishop of Hereford, the Right Rev Anthony Priddis and former Bishop of Bristol, Right Rev Barry Rogerson, were criticized by the Evangelical Alliance, who claimed that changing sex was '... *incompatible with God's will as revealed in Scripture'* and that, according to Genesis, *'God created human beings as male and female'* (Ekklesia, 2005). Such interpretations of the Bible Scriptures served to ostracize some of the Christian subjects of this study, who faced discrimination from within their Church when they sought support during their transition. Let us now examine the ways in which some interpretations of Christian teachings have been instrumental in the ostracism and marginalization of the transsexual parishioner. Here are some of their stories:

Teresa's story:

Teresa is a fully transitioned transsexual woman aged in her late thirties. She was married, but now divorced, and there were several small children, all born during the early years of the marriage. Teresa reported that through her Christian faith, she had found some 'inner strength' to help her cope with the difficulties associated with an acrimonious divorce, the ensuing custody battles for her children, and her own status as a transitioning transsexual woman. Throughout the interview, she referred to her 'Church Family' and this conjured for me a picture of familial support and unity: a group of people upon whom she could depend for acceptance and 'unconditional love'. However, the picture is a very different one. Upon her revelation that she was transsexual and intended to transition, instead of acceptance, Teresa found hostility and ostracism. Here is an excerpt from the interview I carried out with Teresa:

> *Towards the end of that year something else happened and I started realising I had faith and started praying [touching crucifix around her neck] ... at the end of that year I started going to the evangelical church ... three months later ... I did an alpha course ... basically it is instruction in Christianity and Jesus ...*

AB: *So, you joined the evangelical church?*

T: *I joined the church; I was saved in April, 2001.*

AB: *Saved?*

T: *As in, I asked Jesus to ...*

> *I did some online gender tests ... and they all said the same thing — you are transgender — seek help now — your condition is serious ... I sat on it for three weeks and didn't say anything to anyone and after three weeks ... I joined a Christian group online chat room ... a US group, and they kicked me out ... because I was transsexual and they are a right wing Christian group and started posting propaganda describing me as a She-male ...*

> *... I talked to my Church about treatment ... one of the things I told them was that if you take hormones ... it is a diagnostic tool and cross-dressers who think they are transsexual after taking hormones, they don't go back for another appointment, they will throw the hormones away, because they are not transsexual. And I explained that to them ... and they decided that I must not seek treatment ...*

And I had [already] started laser hair removal.

AB: *Your Church decided that you should not transition?*

T: *Yes ... I left that place ... there were a lot of people there that I missed desperately ... but to transition, they don't tend to look on it too well, especially evangelical churches that are quite right wing and so are some of the Pentecostal churches as well.*

At a time, then, when the comfort and support of the 'Church Family' was crucial to Teresa's emotional and what she termed her 'spiritual' health, the church deserted her. Teresa set about trying to find another church that would accept her as a transsexual Christian. Talking of one church she tried, but had refused to accept her, she continued:

T: *I don't think they were trying to judge me, apart from one of the elders. The other three I think were actually sincere, but as a group they were afraid about what was happening inside their church, and I think that's what happened. And it is upsetting, but I don't blame them for it ...*

    So anyway, I went to this [other] church, was welcomed, but I was still in the male role. Then ... I arranged to go and see the rector and talked through it and that's when I found out that they had already been told [by members of Teresa's previous Church group] that this was happening ... and he was fine, he said, 'It's not my place to judge'. So I stayed with that church. I transitioned there ...

Another example of the blatant 'transphobia' evident in the Christian doctrine is the narrative of Jessica, a British transsexual woman who has lived in Hong Kong for many years. She is a Christian and practising Mormon, who, prior to her transition, had regularly attended the Mormon Church, and openly declares that she loves her God and her Church. However, Jessica's change of gender was met with hostility by Church members and she has, according to her own account, been threatened with physical force, barring her from entering the Church building, and this accompanied by verbal abuse and open hostility from Church members, stating: "*... we are not staying here with THAT sitting over there*". Moreover, Jessica was denied the 'sacrament' of bread and wine, and barred from Bible classes and speaking in Church. Finally, she was excommunicated, entirely on the ground of her transsexual status. (Reference: TG2001 Conference Report, University of East Anglia, Norwich, September, 2001: pp.83-84).

Martha's story:

Another informant, Martha, also highlighted the fear of non-acceptance she experienced as a child, growing up in a Catholic home. Here is an excerpt from her interview:

M: *I was raised a Catholic and, ... you know, if you kill somebody, or you rape somebody, or you are a priest who shags the choirboys, say enough Hail Mary's and you get off. And I remember back then, people who were gay or transsexual, that was an excommunication job, ... you know, major, major, major stuff, you know, god created everyone, and loves everyone — except me.*

It was not only the negative reaction of the Catholic Church that Martha feared; she also feared the reaction of her parents, should her transgender status be discovered:

M: *I kept it buried, like you do, like we all do ... because little boys weren't supposed to want to be little girls, and I really believed that if I told my parents they would beat me up and throw me out of the house ...*

Finally, Martha seems also to have harboured a morbid fear of the consequences of the medical profession ever discovering her conviction that she was a 'girl' and not a boy:

M: *And of course, as I learned more ... you know, we are
        talking here mid- to late-sixties, so they used to bang people
        up and feed them drugs and connect them to the mains
        [electricity: Electroconvulsive treatment (ECT)] to try to
        cure them. And the last thing I wanted was a note on my
        medical records saying 'this person is insane' ... I was very,
        very aware of the absolute need not to give anybody the
        slightest clue as to what might be going on, because, you
        know ... I could have been excluded from society ...*

Notwithstanding Martha's fear of the rejection by her parents to her
transgender status, in the event, her fears were, to some extent, unfounded,
even though her revelation, predictably, came as an enormous blow to
them and one which they found difficult to take in:

M: *So, my wife and I went to see Mum and Dad ... later Mum
        came in ... and she cuddled me and said, 'You are still my
        child'. But it was a huge shock, because they had no idea,
        and you know, they thought I'd been a bit suggestible and I
        had got the suggestion from somewhere. They didn't accept
        it; they didn't accept it ...*

While her parents found it hard to accept that their 'son' was going to
become their 'daughter', when it came to Martha's wife and friends, the story
was a different one. Martha talked first about her wife's role in her transition:

M: *I think one of the reasons my transition has been so
        successful in terms of coming to self-acceptance, is [my wife]
        validates me.*

And then her friends:

        *... A lot of people have said, 'Look, we liked and loved you
        before, and we are sure that won't change.*

Samantha's story:

Like many of the subjects of my study, Samantha's early life was dogged by a difficult childhood and the intense loneliness she suffered as a result of her gender identity confusion and the social ostracism and hostility that accompanied this. Like many of my British informants, she reported having been bullied at school: *'I was ostracised, cast out and physically and verbally abused ...'* Samantha recalled her school days thus:

S: *... though I tried my best to fit in and to appear normal, it was obvious to my peers that I wasn't. They accused me of being gay, queer, erm, they used to shout at me and say I was a girl, and they would taunt me and say why didn't I come to school dressed in girls' clothes like the other girls did and why didn't I go to the girls' dressing room rather than the boys', as, erm they beat me and kicked me ... I became very withdrawn, very nervous in myself, unable to relate to anyone and was unable to tell my parents about this ...*

Samantha's problems were compounded by the fact that, although her parents were aware she was being bullied, she felt unable to tell them why; *'I was afraid to tell them ... because I thought they wouldn't understand'.*

The ostracism of her peers continued at college: *'... they knew I was different, I wasn't like them, and they kept away from me',* she reported. This carried on into university where, Samantha said, she was 'very lonely' and had 'virtually no friends'. A subsequent 'nervous breakdown' resulted in Samantha undergoing psychiatric assessment; however, this failed to achieve a satisfactory outcome, because, as she told me, *'... I felt unable to express to the psychiatrist what I was really feeling, that I was a woman, not a man'.*

While the psychiatrists and her parents had tried and failed to find a suitable solution to her distress and confusion, Samantha turned to evangelical Christianity and became a 'born again Christian'. Nonetheless, whereas she found some measure of acceptance within this Christian community, Samantha was not forthcoming when it came to disclosing her gender identity confusion. She told me: *'I was unable to tell them that I was a transvestite because I felt that it was sinful'.*

It is interesting to note that Samantha, along with many of the other transsexual women of this study, initially thought that she was 'merely a cross-dresser' — a transvestite — rather than transsexual.

Pre-transition transsexual women will commonly strive to find a 'cure' for their gender confusion; several of the subjects of this study reported having, as a child 'prayed to God every night' to let them 'wake up a girl', or for some 'miracle cure'. In this regard Samantha was typical. She told me:

S: *... for five or six years I studied the bible and Christian teaching, hoping that I would be cured from where I was and that God would heal me and make me normal ...*

Somewhat predictably, however, no 'miracle cure' was forthcoming.

S: *... I kept falling back into 'dressing', which, according to the bible is a sin and is wrong, and I tormented myself through that ...*

Self-acceptance for Samantha finally came by her late-twenties, with the realisation that she was, indeed, the stereotypically defined 'woman trapped inside a man's body':

S: *I finally came to a place in my life where I accepted what I was and accepted that I wanted to be a woman, that I wasn't really a man, I was a woman in a man's body.*

However, as we have seen in the cases of Teresa and Martha, evangelical Christianity and transsexualism make incompatible bedfellows, and Samantha was well aware of this, as she said: *'Over the course of the next few years I gradually drifted away from the Christian community ...'* having discovered, via the Internet, an organization that offered the facility for transvestites and transsexuals to communicate and attend monthly parties together. This was a significant turning point for Samantha's life, as she reports here:

S: ... *and it was there really that I discovered myself that I*
       first came out to other people that I was a woman and not
       a man, and I discovered that it was like a whole new world
       opening up for me in that I could talk to them and I could
       express myself, I could express my emotions without being
       afraid, and tell people about myself and they would accept
       me and understand me and this was marvellous. It was
       incredible! It was almost miraculous!

Were Samantha's prayers finally answered? Meeting and, for the first time in her life, making friends with other transsexual people led to Samantha becoming informed about which psychiatrists were 'best qualified' in dealing with gender problems and eventually she found the courage to privately consult a psychiatrist who immediately diagnosed gender dysphoria and prescribed hormones. Samantha reflected on the effects of this:

S: *I started taking hormones; I started growing my hair long*
       and started wearing earrings and small pieces of jewellery.
       As the months went by, I started to physically change. People
       noticed the difference in me.

However, the 'difference' people saw in Samantha was not always received with acceptance. Samantha reported that when she told her employers that she was transitioning they immediately threatened her with dismissal, accusing her of 'bringing the company into disrepute'. Furthermore, her parents, worried about the wellbeing of their offspring, sought the advice of the somewhat enlightened minister of their church, who, on realizing that Samantha was a transitioning male-to-female transsexual, was able to reassure them and help them to understand the phenomenon. Samantha's remaining Christian friends, however, were less supportive: they 'disowned' her. And her employers and work colleagues set about victimizing her, to the point that they made her life so unpleasant she resigned, unaware at that time that she could have pursued a case against them under the Sex Discrimination

(Gender Reassignment) Act, that came into force in Britain in May 1999. Samantha recalled her last months at work:

S: *... My employers made life very difficult for me. They gave me the horrible work to do that nobody else wanted to do; they stuck me in a corner and nobody would speak to me. They made my life very unpleasant ... it was awful; it was four months of incredible pressure ... so after four months I bowed to the pressure and resigned ...*

Let us now take a look at Thailand and the experiences of *kathoey* who grow up in a seemingly more tolerant society, when it comes to gender variance, than do transgenders hailing from Western societies.

Kathoey and Thai Law

Thailand's economic standing and its average living standards are much lower than those of Western countries. Hence, Thailand's sex tourism provides a lucrative resource that boosts the country's economy. Although some *kathoey* have enjoyed the privilege and benefits of education, some of the many who have not, often find work in the sex industry as an alternative career to lesser-paid menial work, and yet enjoy at least a tacit social acceptance, in a way that transsexuals in Britain do not. However, caution should be exercised when interpreting data on social acceptance of *kathoey* in Thailand. It is a common misconception that Thailand is a generally accepting and tolerant country. Under Thai law, however, *kathoey* are classified as male and are not permitted to change their name or any legal documents, such as their passport, driver's licence or identity card, whereas in the UK the Gender Recognition Act allows the post-operative transsexual the issuing of a Gender Recognition Certificate in the new gender. While in Britain, transsexuals have for years now been able to change their name and personal legal documents including passport or driver's licence, in Thailand the case of the *kathoey* is a very different one.

The legal and social difficulties that the transgender life brings with it in Thailand, raises questions as to why so many *kathoey* choose this path.

In Thailand, *kathoey* hold no legal status, and no constitutional issue has yet, as far as I am aware, been raised in relation to them (Apirat, 2003). [47] Moreover, at the time of writing there is no law in Thailand that exists to protect *kathoey* and one of the consequences of this is the fact that a *kathoey* has no recourse if they are raped. *Kathoey* then can be sexually violated but unable to bring charges of rape against the perpetrator.

However, at the same time, there exist no specific laws against *kathoey*, although cultural mores appear to make allowances for young *kathoey*. Indeed, over recent years it has become increasingly common to see young 'males' in high schools, which have less strict dress codes, cross-dressing, wearing makeup, long, painted fingernails and feminine jewellery at school. As noted elsewhere in this book, *kathoey* university students regularly wear female attire both on and off campus. Whilst there are no specific laws that discriminate against *kathoey*, it has become increasingly apparent that *kathoey* need and indeed desire legal recognition in their 'true' gender status, that of female or even a 'third sex'. Researching Thai laws regarding *kathoey* proved to be an extraordinarily difficult exercise, not least because, while there exist no laws *against kathoey*, there appear to be no laws in Thailand, whether favourable or not, that apply directly or specifically to them. Moreover, any attempt to elicit information from Thai official channels were thwarted; enquiries to the Thai Interior Ministry and the Thai Justice Ministry were left unanswered.

It is worthy of note that we cannot treat the cases of transgender and the law in the two countries of Britain and Thailand in the same way. Any commentary on the *kathoey*'s place within Thai culture and society has to come from a Thai indigenous perspective. A deep understanding of the case of *kathoey* and Thai law in the context of Thai culture cannot consist of loose generalizations or mere speculation. As I have already stated, *kathoey* would seem to enjoy at least a tacit social acceptance, and certainly a generally tolerant attitude to their transgender expression by Thai society at large. This is evident by the way that transgender in Thailand is, as noted elsewhere in this book, 'celebrated' in some sense, as is observable in the spectacular *kathoey* beauty contests and elaborate

---

47 Apirat Petchsiri, Professor of Law, Chulalongkorn University, personal communication, 2003.

and sometimes highly sophisticated *kathoey* cabaret shows that cater not only to foreign tourists but to Thai audiences as well. Transgender in Thailand, then, is commercialised.

As stated, there are no specific laws in Thailand against *kathoey* (or 'transsexuals'), so for example, it is not illegal for a 'male' to dress and live as a woman. Under Thai law it is not illegal for a person to undergo sex reassignment surgery or other related surgical procedures and nor is it unlawful for Thai surgeons to perform such procedures. *Kathoey* can live and work as female social actors in Thai society without any legal restrictions to expression of their gender — or, rather, transgender — status. Hence it is an everyday observable fact that *kathoey* enjoy the (unwritten) legal/social sanction to assume the female gender role. And this is the case irrespective of whether or not the *kathoey* is a fully transitioned transsexual having undergone sex reassignment surgery. However, *kathoey* hold no legitimate legal status in Thailand, and this means that as far as the law is concerned, they remain male for all intents and purposes.

Furthermore, there is no law in Thailand that prohibits an adolescent *kathoey* from buying hormones in any pharmacy, and neither is it illegal for a pharmacist to sell them and this despite the fact that young *kathoey* are likely unaware of possible adverse effects associated with taking such pharmaceutical drugs. The minimum legal age for a person to undergo sex reassignment surgery without parental consent is eighteen. As noted earlier, Thai surgeons I interviewed told me that the minimum age they accept without parental consent is twenty; between eighteen and twenty with parental consent, for *kathoey* under eighteen the surgeons reputedly absolutely refuse, although I spoke to *kathoey* who reported having undergone sex reassignment surgery at a younger age (Lek, for example, stated that she was sixteen at the time she had such surgery).

Under Thai law, at the age of twenty-one, all 'males' are conscripted to serve in the military; however, *kathoey* are usually rejected on medical or psychiatric, rather than legal grounds. In theory, then, as stated, there exists no Thai law that prevents a person from adopting a change of gender role. However, as noted above, while there is no specific law *against kathoey*, the existing Thai law fails to work *for* them. Gender in Thailand is an immutable legal status that is assigned to a person at birth and cannot be changed.

This leaves *kathoey* precariously placed when it comes to gender-specific laws, which do not cater for them and as, under Thai law, they remain male, this impacts hugely on their lives because they cannot change any legal or personal documents. When required to produce a passport or other travel documentation, their legal status 'male' becomes evident. This means that even post-operative *kathoey* face a dilemma when it comes to overseas travel. This was illustrated by an unfortunate situation that a fully-transitioned *kathoey* friend of mine, in Northern Thailand, experienced when she was invited by a Dutch boyfriend to spend three months with him in Holland. The Dutch Embassy in Bangkok refused three times to issue her a visa, on the grounds that her photograph did not fit the description 'male' on her documents. Such legal anomalies, of course, also mean that *kathoey* are unable to marry 'biological' men, as same-sex marriage in Thailand remains illegal.

In contrast to Britain, Thai transgender culture does not lend itself to political activism and this has meant that any change in law that might otherwise have been effective has not taken place. There have, however, been recorded a small number of attempts by *kathoey* to be legally recognised in their acquired gender; here are two examples. In 1972 a (post-op) *kathoey* applied to have her 'household registration' documents changed to reflect her acquired gender. The Ministry of the Interior refused her application on the ground that gender status is fixed at birth and surgical intervention does not alter this fact. The case was not taken any further (Rakkit, 1997).

Another case occurred in 1981, when a post-op Thai transsexual woman made an application to the Courts for a legal change of gender and for her personal documents to be changed accordingly. The Civil Court, the Court of Appeal and finally the Supreme Court, all ruled against her (Rakkit, 1997). Decades on, the position remains the same; a *kathoey* cannot legally change gender in Thailand. There is no Gender Recognition Act on the *kathoey* horizon. While there exists no legal intervention that prevents transgender status, or behaviour, there is no legislation that protects *kathoey* from institutional discrimination and this causes multitudinous problems that the *kathoey* faces on a regular basis and is impotent to overcome. Now, let us take a look at the ambiguous status that *kathoey* inhabit when it comes to marriage.

Kathoey and marriage

In Thai tradition, monks do not officiate or 'bless' weddings. There are two types of wedding in Thailand: the 'traditional' wedding takes place usually within the bride's family, and is not legally recognised as is the civil marriage. Winter (2002a) states (in common with other researchers) that a *kathoey* cannot legally marry a man, but then confidently contradicts this in another paper (Winter, 2002b, p.4) that male-male marriages 'still occur in some rural areas'. He fails, however, to state the rural areas to which he refers, or to acknowledge the source of this information. In fact, my own research indicates that the traditional wedding serves to provide an alternative for non-normative unions, such as same-sex couples or *kathoey*-'real' man couples. However, the traditional wedding also provides an alternative for male-female couples who do not want a 'legal' or civil marriage because of the legal restrictions that this can bring, for example, women's property rights can be affected by legal and civil marriage. I came across one such a marriage that had taken place between a *farang* biological man and a Thai biological woman, and this seems to be quite common. *Kathoey* cannot legally marry a male because of the very fact that they cannot legally change their gender. One advantage for *kathoey* remaining legally male arises for those who have not undergone genital surgery. Some in this category eventually abandon the *kathoey* life and return to their home villages, marry and father children. Although I have only anecdotal evidence of this, the information comes from various sources within the groups of Thai people I encountered in Thailand. However, I am aware of three male-to-females who legally married each other in Thailand, one a *kathoey* and the other a foreign transsexual, who had legally changed gender from male to female in her own country in the West. In this case, the *kathoey* is legally classified as the husband and her partner, who has undergone genital reassignment surgery but has no breasts and presents as androgynous, is the legal wife. Another fully transitioned *kathoey* told me she was married to an English man. More recently a *kathoey* friend, fully transitioned from male to female, has married a biological Thai man. According to Allyn (2003) there are newspaper reports of a 'traditional' Thai wedding taking place between a *kathoey* and a biological man, or a 'real' man *(poo-chai jing)*, as Thais would term him.

Traditional weddings are permitted to take place in a *'Wat'* (temple) but the rituals undertaken by the monks on such occasions are Buddhist merit-making rituals and are unrelated to the wedding itself (Allyn, 2003). There is, in any case, no such thing as a 'Buddhist' wedding ceremony (Allyn, 2003). It is entirely possible that a 'naïve' *farang* man may think he is legally married to a Thai, when in fact he and is partner have undergone a 'traditional' wedding that has no legal or civil status. One *kathoey* informant of my study reported having married an English man in this way. When asked if her 'husband' was aware of her *kathoey* status, she reported that she was 'not sure' whether or not he knew, but that she had not disclosed her transsexual status to him.

A Thai friend described to me how he and his older gay European partner (to whom he referred as 'my husband') got married in a 'traditional' wedding that his family in Northern Thailand arranged, with himself as the 'bride', wearing white shirt and slacks and bedecked in flowers adorned by his female family members.

Family, friends and other villagers attend the traditional wedding. Monks are regularly invited to such weddings and presented with 'alms' with which they will make merit the following day. The monks are also presented with *'dhak bat'*; these are gifts of flowers, incense or candles for example, and this indicates merit making for the family. Although such a traditional marriage has no legal or civil status, it carries with it for the couple involved as well as their family and friends, considerable meaning and is regarded as a serious and life-long commitment by the couple to each other.

Kathoey and public presentation

Kathoey are free to use the female public toilets in Thailand and habitually do, so the potential 'conduct likely ...' law faced by transsexual women in Britain is not an issue. As far as employment is concerned, *kathoey* may or may not, however, face antipathy in some respects. There appears to be no law against a female-presenting *kathoey* working in high-level employment or public-profile occupations, which bring them in touch with the general public, despite some researchers having noted that such occupations are under-represented by *kathoey*. However, my own observations somewhat refute, or at least do not support Winter's impressions. In Thailand I came across *kathoey* working in public-profile occupations such as travel agents, hospital receptionists and dental assistants. These *kathoey* wore the same uniform as other female employees. Winter states that the Thai Government had 'put barriers in the way of aspiring *kathoey* teachers' (Winter, 2002; no page numbers in original). However, this is either plainly inaccurate or out of date. I interviewed a *kathoey* teacher whose family's socio-economic background could be described as 'wealthy' and 'middle-class' even by European standards. More recently, it has been reported on the internet that *kathoey* flight attendants are now represented in the air travel industry in Thailand (http://www.huffingtonpost.com/2011/12/15/thailand-transgender-flight-attendants_n_1150967.html.)

As a comparison to transsexuals in Britain, *kathoey* probably fair equally when it comes to employment. The fact that they are heavily represented in the sex industry over-simplifies the true picture as broad generalizations and mere speculation based on initial or subjective impressions neglect to take into account important factors. Very few Thai people, certainly as compared to Western and other 'developed countries' or 'First World countries', get the chance of anything more than a basic, rudimentary education. Typically, a child from a lower socio-economic family, if indeed they go to school at all, starts around the age of seven and ends at age twelve. For someone with such limited educational qualifications, sex work is a lucrative opportunity that is not exclusive to *kathoey*. Young women, girls, adolescent boys, youths and even young children (see for example, Montgomery, 2001a; 2001b) from such impoverished backgrounds also engage in sex work, as either prostitutes or rent boys.

The legal and social difficulties that the transgender life brings in Thailand, raises questions as to why so many *kathoey* choose this path. One indication in this regard, as noted earlier in this book, is the fact that as very young children, *kathoey* are made very aware of the transgender phenomenon, as it is observable all around them and easy to recognize. They learn from their families, friends and neighbours that it is possible, and indeed at least tacitly acceptable, to follow a *kathoey* path. It naturally follows, then, that, unlike their British counterparts, who 'suffer' in stigmatized silence, *kathoey* recognize their own transgender status.

One could argue that perhaps the apparently large numbers of *kathoey* in Thailand are due to the tacit social sanctions accorded to them; in other words, Thai society in general, if not in law, allows individual transgender expression some legitimacy. Asking *kathoey* how they came to the awareness that a life career as a transgendered person was open to them, brought the universal response that they had either friends or other family members who were *kathoey*. This was the unanimous response of my Thai sample to the question: *'Roo jahk nai wah sah maht bpree-un pes dai na ka?'* [Translation: 'How did you become aware that you could change your gender?']

Although to the outsider, *kathoey* enjoy the freedom to choose the transgender path, and albeit researchers have, in the past, represented Thailand as a 'safe haven' for non-normative sexual and gender diversity (see for example, Jackson, 1995), on closer examination, Thai attitudes to *kathoey* are not always positive. The following examples of Thai attitudes to *kathoey* I noted in Thailand, illustrate this point:

> *'If you go near kathoey, take extra care because they will steal your watch or your jewellery or your wallet in the street, yes, and sometimes they stab people' (Male Thai, talking about kathoey in Phuket town);*

> *'If you want to interview a kathoey, don't invite them to your hotel room for the interview, because they will stab you and kill you and steal all your valuables; it happens, so be very careful' (Female Thai, Phuket island);*

> *'Gays are alright, but not kathoey. I don't like kathoey. [Being a] kathoey is going too far' (26-year-old Thai hotel waitress, Bangkok).*

However, these attitudes cannot be accepted as universal. The overwhelming majority of Thais, when asked by me, responded, *'it's up to them'*. Matzner (2001, p.23) describes one stereotype of *kathoey* as the 'over-achiever'. This is a strategy adopted by some *kathoey* in an endeavour to compensate for their transgender status and foster social acceptance. While some Thais take a negative attitude to transgender, in that *kathoey* are observed as 'loud', 'aggressive' and violators of the 'polite' behavioural standards so valued in Thai culture, others (particularly female observers) are favourably impressed by *kathoey* who display a talent for chic dress sense, makeup and hair style. A *kathoey* who works hard to achieve high grades in school or university is admired and respected. Tinar talked to me about working hard at school and university because she felt the need to 'prove' herself due to her transgender status. To this end she was awarded scholarships from primary school through to university and achieved the highest grades in her final examinations at university. This led to her running her own tourism business and coffee shop.

While the majority of *kathoey* receive limited education, others, however, who have been fortunate enough to have gone to university, have found that a degree in no way guarantees social acceptance when it comes to finding a job. A twenty-six-year-old university graduate and pre-op *kathoey* I interviewed in Bangkok, told me she had applied for 'many many' jobs after graduating, but had not received a single job offer and she felt that this was due to her *kathoey* status. Significantly, she further reported that should she cut her hair short, wear no makeup and dress as a male, potential employers would accept her. However, this *kathoey* was reluctant to take such a step, as she was very happy being a 'Ladyboy' and would not be happy in the male role, despite remonstrations from her parents: *'Oh, why, why, why be a kathoey? You have a degree, you can have a good life as a man, why do you want to be a kathoey?'* She finally found work as a freelance makeup artist. Another *kathoey* I met, was well aware of the lack of employment opportunities that accompany transgender in Thailand and for this reason chose to live and work in the male role. On first sight, Onni looks like a young, effeminate gay man. His walk is more stereotypically 'feminine' than masculine, and his mannerisms are soft and effeminate. Onni's speaking voice and laugh are higher up the vocal register than that of a conventionally 'masculine' man. As he does not take hormones, he has the body type of a male but I detected that he was wearing a little subtle makeup; face powder and lip-gloss. His hair is not cut short, but neither is it very long, and he wears it pulled back from his face in a hair clip. I met Onni in an Internet café where he worked. Curious as to his gendered status, I begged his forgiveness before enquiring: *'Khun bpen kon Ladyboy chai mai ka?'* [Trans: Are you a Ladyboy?], to which he readily answered, with a wide smile, *'Chai ka!'* [Trans: Yes!]. Interestingly, indeed significantly, this male-presenting effeminate young man used the female-specific polite particle 'ka'. As noted previously, the polite particle used by males is 'krup', and the fact that Onni used 'ka' is indicative of his self-identity as a female. Fascinated by this young man's self-presentation, I asked if I could interview him, and he excitedly agreed forthwith! Speaking in English, I asked Onni if he felt himself to be a woman inside, and he said that he did, *'one hundred percent!'* Asked when he had started to feel like that he replied, *'I feel like that when I am baby ... about three or four years.'* I asked him if, when he was a little boy, he played with dolls, to which he replied (in English), *'Uh huh, yes, I play with doll, I play with girl. But someone tell me don't play with the girl ...'*, adding, however, that while his parents knew he was playing with dolls and girls, they showed no opposition to this. Onni reported that he had never worn feminine clothes, even though inside he felt like a woman, he only ever wore tee-shirt and jeans, *'like a man'*, adding, *'Many Ladyboy* [are] *like me, have many, many'*. I asked Onni if he had ever had a problem trying to get a job. Speaking in English, he replied:

> *No, because in Thai, in Thai social [society], they like to have a man and they accept [him as a man]. [But even] if I am thinking like a woman, I look like a man. But if some Ladyboy, they change to be a lady, Thai social or the company ... they don't accept.*

This *kathoey*, then, well aware of the social problems that can arise for the feminine 'Ladyboy', took the strategic plan to live and work in the male role, in order to avoid jeopardising his career prospects. As far as his sexual orientation is concerned, Onni told me that he had been in a relationship with his 'heterosexual' boyfriend for the past three years, and was accepted in the relationship as a woman. As noted by Sinnott (2004), sexual orientation and gender identity in Thailand are understood in terms that do not fit Western concepts of these indicators. Therefore imposing Eurocentric sensitizing concepts onto 'other cultures' can only fail to explain certain concepts. In Thailand, for example, *toms* are regarded as male because *toms* form same-sex relationships with *dees*. From a Western perspective, such relationships are 'lesbian'. However, *toms* and *dees* reject this term as derogatory.

I would like now to highlight the diverse reactions from parents upon discovery of their 'son's' *kathoey* status.

Kathoey and their families

So far I have attempted to illustrate the ways in which gender expression is prevalent in Thai society and the implications of this for 'gender variant' individuals in Thailand. Next, I give, through some *kathoey* stories the implications of a family's 'son' becoming a 'daughter'. Let's start with Lek.

Lek, worked as a cabaret dancer, and like many other *kathoey* working in cabaret, had sometimes subsidised her salary by prostitution with *farang* men. She reported having taken hormones since the age of thirteen, and undergone sex reassignment surgery at the age of sixteen or seventeen, which she paid for herself. Lek reported having felt like a girl from a very young age. Although Lek's mother and siblings accepted her as a *kathoey*, her narrative suggests that her father was not so agreeable at first. Speaking in her broken English, she explained:

> *I had problem with my Papa, because Papa not like me being a lady. Him want I be the man and work very hard for him ... I can work very hard, but inside me don't change, I want to be lady ... When I come to work I have money for operations, I do myself and I go back [home] and Papa OK ...*

As with other parents of *kathoey*, Lek's father, when faced with a *fait accompli*, accepted his new 'daughter'. Like many *kathoey* working in the sex industry, Lek's relatively high income enabled her to send money home to the family and to buy the family a house, making the family's socio-economic status rise from low to comparatively high, and Lek believes that it is for this reason, that her father is now accepting of her *kathoey* status. This corresponded to the narrative of other *kathoey* sex workers to whom I spoke; whilst their parents knew they were working as prostitutes, they turned a blind eye as long as their offspring sent money home. Other *kathoey* prostitutes had told their parents they were working in a restaurant or in some other such benign occupation.

Pui's story:

When I met Pui, she was twenty-four years old and was working in a hotel and beach bar, which she jointly owned with Steve, a Western man in his early sixties,[48] and Tom, her younger, Thai boyfriend. As a teenager Pui had run away from her home in Northern Thailand, to escape the brutal cruelty she had suffered at the hands of her parents because of her transgender status. Pui recalled as a small child, her father expressing his ambition for her to train as a soldier or a police officer when she grew up.

Pui: My father wanted me to be a man, go to army school ... or
police school ...

Despite her father's ambitions for Pui (to train as a soldier or police officer), Pui harboured the deep desire to be a girl. Speaking in English, she recalled the time, aged 'about seven or eight', when her parents caught her playing with a doll and singing 'like a girl'. Here is her verbatim account:

> *... But one time I go get ... doll and Mama not know ... and*
> *then I play, talk with doll, I play with doll like a girl [plays]*
> *and I take a pin for long hair and put in my hair and look*
> *like girl ... and I take my sister's clothes and do things like*
> *dancing like lady ... and I put doll in pocket and play and*
> *sing and Papa he put my hands like this [shows how he tied*

---

48 By stating the disparity between Pui's and Steve's ages, I am not by any means making a judgement or suggesting some sort of impropriety, but merely describing aspects of the relationship between Steve and Pui and Tom.

*her wrists together] ... and he took me to a tree and tied me
to the tree and put ants on me ...*

Pui recalled another incident of cruelty, this time at the hands of her
mother, who was on frequent occasions, insensibly intoxicated:

Pui: *I go play with girls and I come back and when cooking
finished I make like theatre like cabaret show. I dance, I
sing. Mama come back and she see and she take me and say
'cannot' and Mama drunk ...
And she do like this [tied hands together at the wrists] and
put me in pond ... in water, in pool. And she say will do
again if I do that [play like a girl] ... and Mama say, 'oh,
have crocodile, crocodile' and say, 'crocodile eat you, eat
you if you do like lady, crocodile not like lady, crocodile
like man, and if you be man crocodile not eat you', so after
that I don't do any more. Now I scared of crocodile, I don't
like to see crocodile any more and I don't like to go in water,
I don't like swimming, make me scared, I not do any more.*

Perhaps unsurprisingly, for several years after she ran away from home,
Pui had no contact with her family. She told me: '*... I don't contact the
family, they think I die*'. Pui described how, at one point before she met
Steve and Tom, her distress was so great that she placed a noose around
her neck and tried to hang herself.

Pui: *Inside I lady, but nobody want me, before Tom and Steve,
nobody want me, I not happy. I think inside I want to make
lady, but I think nobody want me ... before [as a male] I
have pain, but now I so happy. And now thinking like lady,
everything lady ...*

Fortunately, not all lack of familial acceptance in Thailand is expressed
in such extreme and brutal ways as that of Pui's parents. When I met Pun,
she was twenty-three-years-old and a post-op *kathoey*. Like other *kathoey*,

she had felt herself to be a girl from a very young age. She recalled the time that she was sitting next to her mother, who accidentally touched Pun's thigh and felt the hormone patch she was wearing. Here is an excerpt from Pun's narrative (this part of the interview was conducted in English):

Pun: *She touch me ... and 'Oh!'— she know I have something*
       already and know about this and don't talk with me all the
       day and then ... she say 'You know, that bad for you'... and I
       think what shall I do, because I feel scared, and actually, my
       mother, she like a friend of me, and she very funny — yes! I
       can ask some advice from her, anything, but her very quiet
       [after discovering the hormone patch] and I never see her
       like this before ... and I think maybe I do something very,
       very wrong ...

Unlike Pui's parents, Pun's mother did not appear to Pun to be angry, nor did she punish Pun, but remonstrated with her that she had more chance of a happy and successful life as a male in Thai society rather than a female or *kathoey*:

       ... she don't tell me but I know because her face is not angry,
       but quiet, and I feel scared ... she don't say she don't like
       but she think my life be sad life and she said 'You have to
       think about if you feel like this, how can you have happy
       life?'... she talk like that ... that I have to think about it ...
       because it make things more difficult ... she afraid I cannot
       have good life.

Wan's story:
    As discussed earlier, in his study of 'presentations of self in everyday life', Goffman's 'dramaturgical approach' describes the presentation of self in terms of 'performance' of the 'social actor' and situates the actor within the broader social context. Interaction, then, is viewed as a 'performance' that is shaped by the social actor's social environment. In this way, the social actor seeks to make 'impressions' that are harmonious with the

desired achievements or outcome of the actor. Performance in everyday life is something that is highly valued in Thailand. Falling short of this Goffmanesque ideal can result in the discrediting of the social actor/ performer by Thai society at large. Creditable everyday appearances, then, together with public performance are crucial elements when it comes to Thai social acceptance of *kathoey*. Like other *kathoey*, Wan, a graduate student in her early twenties placed a lot of importance on her everyday appearance. It seemed her sense of self-respect and self-worth was dependent upon her successful self-presentation. I experienced Wan as a young woman; she was in fact a pre-op transsexual woman, and had been taking hormones since she was in her late-teens. She reported:

> *Wan:* *I try to make everything beauty, everything beauty on my body because I think that nowadays [Thai] society is judging by appearance — I don't think that I am a woman, but I think that I must dressing my body beautiful all the time because I don't want people to discredit me. And I feel very concerned about looks, about appearance.*

Wan reported that she felt fortunate that her family accepted her unconditionally, and the fact that she is transgender made no difference:

> *Wan:* *I think I am so lucky that my surrounding people give a good image of me. And surrounding people don't do anything to hurt me. I think family is important for transgender people.*
> *AB:* *Yes, because not all kathoey are — ?*
> *Wan:* *[interjecting] — not all kathoey have acceptance from their family.*

I asked Wan about her friends from school, and her university friends. She told me:

> *Wan:* *Yes, my friend, in my apartment accepting about my identity ... and my Ajahn [Trans: university lecturers], they all accept me.*

However, Wan's experience of being *kathoey* in Thailand has not always been positive. When I asked her if she had ever had ever experienced antagonism because of her *kathoey* status; she recalled an incident that occurred in which she suffered a 'spoilt' identity, when she was called up for a medical examination to asses her physical fitness for conscription for service as a soldier in the Thai army. Wan recalled the humiliating situation in which she found herself, standing naked, on the occasion of her army selection medical examination:

Wan: ... *many soldier talk, so rude, so impolite to me ... and in this situation, have a doctor to, er, to judge who is a perfect body, who is illness — and I have just to be illness people psycho ... mental illness [categorized as mentally ill].*

AB: *Is that what they said?*

Wan: *Yes, they try to, I try to avoid this until the next year, because I am a student, but the next time I must go to this situation and have a check my name, every year ... till I am finished studying. And the last year, I go, and the doctor wanted to check my breasts. Kathoey must be nude, take all the clothes off, the doctor have authority to touch the body of kathoey. Sometimes the doctor is very impolite, because he is a man, he touch my breasts, he do the vagina of the kathoey who do [has undergone] sexual reassignment. He has the authority, and me too I must leave [take] my clothes off.*

An interpretation of Wan's report suggests that the authority of the army medical officer means that he can physically or sexually abuse or humiliate the *kathoey*. This narrative, then, serves as an illustration of the covert non-acceptance of the transgender phenomenon in Thailand. Moreover, while Thai surgeons and psychiatrists suggest that the transgender phenomenon is not classified as a psychiatric disorder, Wan's narrative contradicts this, in that *kathoey* are rejected on psychiatric grounds by the Thai army. However, Wan was fortunate in that, as a well-educated and articulate person, she had the confidence to approach the commanding officer of the army medical department, and to implore him not to record her on her medical record as being 'mentally ill'. She told me:

Wan: I talk to the Head of the soldier, that 'I want to study for
a PhD ... and the doctor should not judge me as a mental
illness, because it is hard for me to get a job ...' and so, lucky
that he understand me and he go to talk with the doctor
to recommend that I have different size of breasts [in other
words, a physical, rather than a mental condition].

While Wan expressed her relief that she was classified as having a
physical rather than a 'mental' condition, her categorization as such on
the ground of different sized breasts did nothing to protect her right
to privacy, as legally she remains male, with a male name, and so is
instantly identifiable as *kathoey* and would ordinarily and automatically
be categorized as mentally ill by the Thai army. Wan, like other *kathoey*, is
constantly negotiating her transgendered embodiment. It is indeed ironic
that while *kathoey* are allowed some legitimacy in Thailand, in that they
are freely able to express their gender variance in everyday situations, that
legally they remain unequivocally male. Such irony is compounded when
we consider the ways that the transgender phenomenon in Thailand
is otherwise celebrated. Next I explore the celebration of Thailand's
'Ladyboys' within the context of the Miss Alcazar beauty contest I
attended in Pattaya in 2004.

Thailand's ultimate celebration of transgender: The *Kathoey* Beauty contest

The fundamental distinction between the expressions of transgender
in Britain and Thailand is that whereas the transsexual woman in Britain
will commonly strive to be 'stealth', that is, blend into society and be
recognised as a genetic woman, in Thailand the transgender phenomenon
is, to some extent, celebrated. Indeed, the celebration of transgender in
Thailand can be observed at the *kathoey* 'beauty contests' that regularly
take place in various parts of the country. In Pattaya, for example, 'Miss
Alcazar' and 'Miss Tiffany' beauty contests are held annually at their
respective cabaret venues. I attended the 2004 'Miss Alcazar' Contest,
where Goffman's notion of 'dramaturgy' is brought to life on the stage.
The following vignette, taken from my fieldnotes serves to capture the

exhibition and cultural celebration of gender diversity that is particular to, and displayed through the beauty pageants of Thailand.

Miss Alcazar: Pattaya, March 2004 — A vignette

The auditorium was packed to full capacity. An air of excited expectation swept through the audience as the curtains drew back, revealing a large stage, the set elaborate and spectacular. The MC announced the start of the contest. Who would become the new Miss Alcazar? In celebration of 'Amazing Thailand's' transgender phenomenon, this lavish artistic production began.

Contestant Number One glided elegantly across the stage. She wore a long white, sparkling evening dress and a disc, identifying her as contestant number '1', like a bracelet on her left wrist. As she paused centre stage, the MC introduced her to the audience, asking her Name, Age, Height, Weight and occupation as Number One smiled brightly, scanning the audience. Her responses to the MC's questions came with a masculine, lower, deeper register voice that juxtaposed incongruously with her highly feminine appearance and coy demeanour. As she proceeded to walk closer to the audience, enthusiastic, rapturous applause followed ...

Number One contestant was a vision of 'feminine beauty'. Makeup, carefully, expertly applied, long hair sophisticatedly styled up and back off her face, her white, sparkling evening dress hugging her womanly figure. Notably, her skin tone was pale; a Thai ideal of 'Western' style beauty.

I made a mental note: "She is going to win!" Number One is going to win.

The other 59 contestants were introduced, one by one, gliding across the stage, smiling, as they responded to the MC's questions as to their age, height, weight, and occupation.

Some two hours later, the judges had deliberated and it was time to announce the winner — Number One was Number One — Miss Alcazar 2004!

Paradoxically, then, Thai society simultaneously accepts and rejects transgender, first of all by 'celebrating' and displaying to a public audience the 'feminine' beauty of the *kathoey*, then rejects her by rendering her invisible where the law is concerned. A *kathoey* contestant in the beauty contest is judged on the extent of her 'feminine' beauty and her 'femininity'. The winner crowned Miss Alcazar is the one whose 'presentation of self' is most convincingly 'feminine'. Skin tone is a factor that looms large in this judgement. I found that many Thais admire white skin, so the paler the *kathoey* beauty contestant's skin tone the more merit points she is awarded by the judges. As she plays the 'feminine' role, her self-identity is validated by her success at conquering her birth gender and she enjoys the triumph of becoming 'Miss Alcazar', the most 'beautiful woman' in Pattaya. Indeed, as some would opine, some *kathoey* are 'more beautiful than "real" women'. However, the *kathoey* beauty contestant's created illusion of femininity is shattered when she speaks, revealing a discord between feminine beauty and masculine voice. Hence she suffers a 'spoilt' identity.

Let us now explore the diverse reactions to transgender that I observed among Western tourists and Thais in Pattaya, one of the sex tourism centres of Thailand.

East meets West:
Reactions to the transgender phenomenon in Thailand

There are strikingly different attitudes and responses to the Western transsexual woman that I observed, between Thai people and Western (usually) sex tourists. During my fieldwork studies in Thailand I spent some time in Pattaya, viewed by some as the 'sex tourism centre' of Thailand. As in other tourist cities in Thailand, *kathoey* are abundant and can be found in the bars and cabarets everywhere. I stayed in the house of a British friend, Gill. (Recall Gill is a fully transitioned transsexual woman and who had lived in Thailand for approximately fourteen years). Gill underwent her transition while living in Bangkok, which was relatively straightforward and unproblematic, when compared to the sometimes, tortuous transitioning process experienced by contemporary transsexuals in Britain. While I was staying with Gill in Pattaya, a number of other Western transsexual women, in Thailand for sex reassignment and various related surgeries, spent time at the house. As a research student studying transgender, this was a 'researcher's paradise'. For me, being in public with this group of British transsexual women was an ideal opportunity to collect valuable data via the research method of observation. In high-quality restaurants, service staff were attentive yet otherwise the transgender status of my companions seemed to go unnoticed. At other times, while the service staff paid little or no attention other than to serve them, other Western customers I observed in the restaurant would be taking a surreptitious sideways glance.

At a height of approximately six feet five inches (195 cm), Gill has become accustomed to attracting a lot of attention in public. However, this attention is either positive or negative, depending upon the context and whether it came from Thais or Western foreigners. 'Walking Street' is a pedestrianized street located in the middle of the tourist area in Pattaya, where every night the sex tourist can be sure to find the company of young Thai prostitutes, trying to earn enough to fulfil the cultural imperative to send money home to their parents in rural villages throughout Thailand. All manner of sexual preference is catered for in Pattaya's Red Light district. Observing the responses of Western tourists to British transsexual women in Pattaya revealed the very negative cultural values they brought with them from the West, and these contrasted strikingly with those of Thai people I observed. *Farang* appeared to regard Gill as some kind of freak. Unable to hide their facial expressions these ranged from repugnance to ridicule; their verbal expressions ranging from whispered mutterings of *'Look, look, look ...'* while digging an elbow in the ribs of their companion, to violently abusive comments like: *'Look at the fuckin' size o' that!'*

While the British male tourist who said this was, in all probability, referring to Gill's striking height, his expletive and attitude echoed attitudes to transgender prevalent among Western tourists in Pattaya. On another occasion, I was in Bangkok with a group of friends, including one *kathoey*, when, for the purposes of my research, we visited a Red Light district to observe *kathoey* in small cabaret bars. Taking the elevator, three British men aged in their mid- to late-twenties proceeded to make offensive, sarcastic and indeed intimidating remarks in reference to our *kathoey* friend: *'Oh, he looks like a nice girl, doesn't he?'* However, on occasion, it was seemingly 'respectable' Western tourists who would display negative attitudes. On one such occasion, I was in the company of six British transsexual women, in a restaurant in Pattaya. A group of three British couples sitting at a nearby table could be seen sniggering at the transwomen in our company. The very positive attitudes and responses of Thai people, on the other hand, could not have been more contrasting from those of Western tourists. Reacting to Gill's elegant, statuesque figure, Thais would call out, '*Soong, soong*' (translation: very tall); or '*soo-ay mahk*' (very beautiful); or, in English, '*Number One Sexy lady!*' often accompanied with a request to have a photograph taken with Gill. It is noteworthy that in places located outside of Red Light districts in Thailand, Gill commands little attention, neither positive nor negative.

In Britain there exists a legal and social structure that ostensibly supports or 'accepts' transsexuals on a legal level and a system of transition makes it possible to change legal documents and successfully achieve a 'change' of sex. However, when it comes to British social attitudes both in this country and in Thailand, these fall short almost to the point of making a mockery of the legal system that supposedly accepts and 'protects' the transgendered person. In Thailand, on the other hand, where there is no social or legal structure that supports *kathoey*, on an individual level, they enjoy a different kind of acceptance, albeit a limited one. We cannot assume, however, that individual freedom to express one's gender in any way amounts to a social acceptance in a legal or 'formal' sense. Notwithstanding this assertion, in a society such as Thailand, where it is so relatively unproblematic (as compared to Britain) to achieve a 'change of gender' and live the life of a *kathoey*, this might perhaps explain why there is such a proliferation of transgender in that country; they 'become' a *kathoey*, because they know they can, and, notwithstanding the case of Pui, this situation sits in stark contrast to the little boy growing up in Western society, where the possession of 'feminine' traits has been so scorned and stigmatized, to the degree that the child learns to internalize at a very early age, the knowledge that boys are, incontrovertibly boys and to display feminine behaviour or express the desire to be a girl would be, unequivocally, sheer folly, and the consequences, potentially catastrophic.

By examining the tensions between the conflicting and interactive elements that exist between the transgendered individual and society at large in the two very different settings of Britain and Thailand, where attitudes and practices regarding sex, the body and sexual orientation differ so strikingly, what emerges is the need to look carefully at the wider cultural pictures. Examinations of the public/formal as set against the private/informal in these two countries highlights the tension prevalent in the social settings of both countries as to what people *say* they do and what they *actually* say and do. While Britain then, fosters 'acceptance' and 'tolerance' when it comes to the law, in fact it is more likely to be mocking, critical, intolerant and un-accepting when it comes to the transsexual person. Thai law, on the other hand, is intolerant of *kathoey* in that it renders them legally invisible; yet Thai culture and society in general, express acceptance, and hence facilitating the high visibility of this phenomenon. The exception to this is Pui's parents. Sometime after my interview with Pui, her father visited her at the beach hotel where she works and co-owns. It had been several years since she had seen him and her family had thought she was dead. Proudly introducing me to her father as her *farang* friend, a doctoral student, she admonished him to '*wai*' me, which he did, and with a wide smile Pui told me, '*My father is happy now that he has a daughter*'. However, Pui's father's delight in his 'new' daughter was likely to derive from her elevated social status as the co-owner of a flourishing business and the fact that she was now able to fulfil the cultural imperative to financially support her parents in their later years. Pui no longer works in the sex industry. She is fulfilling her filial duty to send money home. When I asked *kathoey* prostitutes if their parents were aware of their occupation, all of them told me either that their families thought they worked in a restaurant or some other 'respectable' job, or that their parents did know what they were doing but did not raise any objection because they sent money home to them. A further illustration of this is Lek's story in this chapter.

So, what does all of this say about the wider cultural perspectives of people in England and Thailand? In order to answer this question we need to situate it within the terms of the opposing social settings of England and Thailand, and then examine the problem holistically. In order to explore the general view of sexuality and gender and what is and is not taboo, it helps to place these within the respective religious foundations prevalent in these two cultures. In doing so we can highlight how the private individual is able to express him- or herself in the public domain.

The predominant 'religion' in Thailand is Buddhism, and, as a philosophy, as discussed elsewhere in this book, this is more 'accepting' and 'benign' than, for example, Christianity, the traditional religion in the UK. In contrast to Buddhism, Christianity is a more prescriptive religion that is expressed in terms of sin and guilt and the resultant stigma that attaches to such an ethos. This is borne out to a limited extent by the stories of two out of the three English Christian transsexual women informants, discussed in this chapter. Teresa's Church not only unceremoniously excluded her from attending services, but also told her unequivocally that she could not transition. Even the American Christian online group that Teresa had turned to for emotional support, first condemned her, then persecuted her by publishing what Teresa described as 'propaganda' about her on the website, condemning her as a 'She-male'. This mistreatment was entirely due to Teresa's transgender status. Although the parents of Samantha, received some support from their Church minister, that enabled them to more fully understand their transsexual daughter's gender discord, upon disclosure of her transgender status, Samantha herself lost friends from within the Christian community. While Martha reported no discrimination on the part of the Catholic Church, nevertheless she spent her childhood in fear of excommunication by the Church and rejection from her parents, and this is a real fear for the majority of the British transsexual women of this study.

What we are left with then, in comparing social acceptance of transgender in Britain and Thailand is a lining up of covert and overt tolerance with covert and overt *in*tolerance. In Thailand, society at large seemingly displays overt tolerance, yet Thai law expresses covert *in*tolerance. In Britain, where the law displays overt tolerance, when it comes to society at large, transsexual people typically experience covert *in*tolerance. All of the British subjects of this study came up against varying degrees of familial opposition to change. Despite the generally held view that Thailand is tolerant to transgender, I found widely variable levels of social acceptance and non-acceptance and familial acceptance or opposition to the 'son' taking the *kathoey* career path. What we are left with, then, is the existence in Thai society of widely disparate levels of acceptance.

CONCLUSION

In this book I set out to investigate and compare the social worlds and lived experiences of transsexual women in England and *kathoey* in Thailand. The findings that emerge from the data indicate the very rich comparisons that exist between the experiences of the transgender phenomenon in the two countries. I wanted to investigate what the process of changing gender involves for the English and Thai transfolk, and the motivations that push individuals across the gender borders. I found that motivations to change gender differed between the two groups. In England, male to female transsexuals were fully masculinized, mature men before the start of their transition. This made transitioning all the more difficult as they tried to transform a mature male body into a female form. However, despite such hurdles to overcome, for many of my English informants, it came to the point of despair when, they reported, it was a case of 'transition or die'. This was because the need to express, openly and legitimately, their 'true' gender identity became overwhelmingly critical and imperative.

In Thailand, although they are legally regarded as *male* throughout their lives, *kathoey* have never been physically *men*. The reason for this is that the masculinizing process of maturation is halted at puberty by the ingestion of female hormones, acquired without the need for medical consultation. However, my findings suggest that while some *kathoey* felt that they were 'true ladies' others were motivated to change only their outwardly visible image, seeking to look like 'beautiful' women, yet, defying the increasingly antiquated binary concept of gender, to retain the ultimate insignia of maleness: their male genitals. For others the *kathoey* life seemed to offer a relatively well-paid career as cabaret performers and/or prostitutes.

I also questioned what is involved in the process of transition in England and Thailand, and my findings also suggest that the processes are very different.

There is a marked contrast between the strategies for 'gender migration' that were employed by these two groups. While in England the transsexual child struggled with their cross-gender identity and strove to keep secret their cross-dressing practices, the *kathoey* child generally experienced a facilitating environment, where transgender is understood as one more aspect of humanity that constitutes a paying back of *karmic* debt.

The fundamental problem with the NHS system that transwomen complained about was the arrogant attitude of psychiatrists at gender identity clinics. All of the transwomen of this study who went to Thailand for surgery made the decision entirely due to either the humiliating way they had been treated at gender identity clinics or because of the stories of such treatment they heard from others. One psychiatrist I interviewed stated that a successful real life experience is essential before sex reassignment surgery and gave an example of the transsexual person who had regretted going to Thailand for surgeries and wanted to change back. Such mistakes would be less likely to occur if the Western doctors learned from Thai doctors and adopted a more patient-centred approach to the care of transsexual patients. Respondents reported that, in stark contrast, Thai doctors were unfailingly courteous and treated them with due respect as intelligent, rational adults.

Gill's story of transition in Thailand exemplified the merits of a 'patient-centred' approach to changing gender. However, Gill's account also highlights a dual system operating in Thailand that is made up of two distinct, opposing elements; this is a very important factor in an analysis of the gender changing facilities in that country. While young *kathoey* with whom I spoke had never consulted an endocrinologist with regard to taking oestrogen tablets, Gill's programme of transition included careful monitoring of the hormone treatment she was given. The important factor here is that Gill was paying well for the care of her doctors, who charge foreign patients more than they charge Thai patients. *Kathoey* hailing from impoverished backgrounds do not have the luxury of such care at their disposal. They simply bought the hormones after a brief consultation with a pharmacist, whose duty of care seemed not to extend to young *kathoey* customers. The exception to this related to intravenous hormones, when *kathoey* consulted a doctor to administer the drugs. Despite admonishments from doctors not to overdose on hormones, consulting different doctors for the injections easily achieved overdosing. Overdosing on hormones exaggerated the feminizing process, and this appealed to *kathoey,* especially those working in the sex industry, whose goal was to look as stereotypically feminine as possible. For *kathoey,* no 'real life experience' is required, for as one doctor noted, they carry out their own real life experience, it is what they do all their lives.

By contrast, in England, transsexuals attending a gender identity clinic are required to live 'full-time' in the female gender role *before* hormone treatment is commenced. The doctor has the authority to control the transition. Thus the transsexual patient is disempowered under the gender identity clinic regime. According to reports from my informants in England, the transsexual person is expected to obediently and unquestioningly accept the doctor's assessment; otherwise they risk the withholding of treatment. The exception to this was via the private route in Britain. Respondents reported having hormones prescribed at the first private consultation with a psychiatrist. One psychiatrist in private practice, who prescribed hormones at the first consultation, has been the subject of investigation by the British Medical Council when some of his patients regretted changing gender after undergoing full sex reassignment surgery in Thailand and wanted to change back.

A patient-centred perspective serves to empower the individual by facilitating the process while at the same time allowing the 'patient' jurisdiction over decisions as to pace and timing of each stage. For instance, the real life experience would be better conducted at the transsexual person's own pace and discretion. The decision to 'dress' full-time or not could be left with the transsexual person themselves. The requirement to undergo the real life experience and live full-time in the female role before hormones are prescribed means that transsexual women are easily 'read' in public and thus left open to the risk of abuse.

There are social and legal incompatibilities that transfolk experience in these two countries. My findings suggest that social acceptance was either overt or covert, depending upon the country and the context. Social acceptance of transgenders in England depended upon the individual's ability to 'pass' as female. Paradoxically, while the transsexual woman in England suffered discrimination and other forms of non-acceptance at street level, she finds some protection now from the law. The Gender Recognition Act means that sex category assigned at birth is no longer immutable where UK law and rights of transsexuals is concerned. Legally, transsexuals in Britain are now recognised as belonging to their new gender and this offers them some protection under the Gender Recognition Act, 2004. It is now legislatively recognised that gender identity resides within the personal and inner sense of a person's self-identity. Transsexuals are now able to apply for a Gender Recognition Certificate and to marry partners of the same 'birth' sex as themselves. However, as I have highlighted, for *kathoey* in Thailand, the picture is a different one. While the Thai culture espouses the more relaxed '*mai bpen rai*' [Trans: It doesn't matter, no worries, no problem] attitude, and an understanding that *kathoey* status comes from past life *karma*, gender is immutable and under Thai law, *kathoey* are categorised as male for all of their lives. Somewhat ironically, while Thai law does not cater to *kathoey* status, Thai society celebrates the transgender phenomenon, as evidenced by the Beauty Contests that take place all over the country.

Incontrovertibly, there is a need for a greater understanding of these groups of people, in both countries investigated here. Medical evidence and the data collected from medical professionals in both England and Thailand provided an insight into the varying approaches, integrity and sensibilities of doctors working in the field of transsexualism. There is a vital need for medical support, especially in relation to the psychiatric evaluation of patients to make sure that they have the mental strength and stability to successfully undertake such a momentous life change. Drawing on the narratives of subjects gathered through qualitative interviews, I have argued that a change of gender is relatively easy to achieve in a more patient-centred and facilitating environment. Gill's private treatment programme in Bangkok was carefully monitored, and the standard of care provided for her was exemplary. Moreover, she was spared the patronizing attitude that transsexual women trying to transition on the NHS reported as their experience.

The differing cultural, religious, medical and social attitudes that prevail in the two countries impact on the ways that transgendered embodiment is experienced and negotiated. The social worlds of transgendered individuals in England and Thailand contrast markedly. My findings point to the impact on the ways that the transgender phenomenon is experienced in the two countries, results from the different cultural, religious, medical and social attitudes that prevail. The two very different religious philosophies affect the levels of social acceptance prevailing in England and Thailand. Findings indicate the cultural differences that result from a 'moralistic' attitude in the United Kingdom and the *'mai bpen rai'* attitude of Thailand, impact on the personal experiences of transgendered individuals.

Aspects of the transitioning processes in the two countries indicate that neither system of transition is ideal. From the point of view of the transwomen in UK, the NHS road to transition is dogged by the negative experiences of attending the gender identity clinic for psychiatric assessment and what was perceived as a patronizing attitude of the psychiatrists who treat them. Equally, from my perspective as an observer, it is clear that the Thai system fails to protect young 'boys', who want to turn themselves into 'girls', from the risks of taking unregulated hormones that are served over the counter to any child who has the money to pay for them. Paradoxically, Thai surgeons offer a first class service to international patients who consult them for sex reassignment and related surgeries. Moreover, sex reassignment surgery is readily available to *kathoey* who can afford to pay for it. However, by failing to adequately establish the mental health of the patient, Thai surgeons have operated on foreign patients who have later regretted undergoing sex reassignment surgery. Hence, I would conclude that there are lessons that each country can learn from each other when it comes to the medical and psychological support services offered to transsexual patients.

There has been a paucity of sociological-anthropological research on the different ways that transgender is experienced in different cultures. I hope that my work here has served to address such a gap in the knowledge. As far as I am aware, it is the first study that investigates the way that transgender is experienced in England and Thailand. This work also highlights the key role of medical professionals in shaping the experience of transition in these two very different countries. It does this by examining the differing approaches to changing gender that are adopted by British and Thai doctors. I have also demonstrated how belonging to these different national cultures can shape the life and transitioning experiences of those persons — virtual women — who find themselves negotiating the transgender experience in England and Thailand.

AFTERWORD

A Third Sex?

As it's title indicates, Richard Totman's (2003) book, *The Third Sex*, categorizes *kathoey* as not male and not female, but a third sex, and at the end of my study I would concur with Totman's evaluation. From my observations, *kathoey* are not physically like Thai women, and neither do they remotely resemble Thai men. Given there is so much variety it is difficult to generalize. However, it is intriguing that while the average height of a Thai woman is 157.5 cm and that of a Thai man, 168.6 cm, the majority of the *kathoey* I met were at least the same height as myself (170 cm), frequently rather taller. Most, if not all the Thai men I encountered were shorter than myself. Another feature of *kathoey* that distinguishes them is the shape of their legs. Almost without exception, *kathoey* I observed, whether stage performers or in everyday occupations, had long, shapely, feminine legs. When I mentioned this observation to a (Western, male) researcher, the matter-of-fact comment came: 'Oh, it's the hormones'. I am not convinced.

So, how does one, indeed can one, explain this phenomenon? The *kathoey*, that mysterious and charismatic creature, who resides 'betwixt and between' in gender — a third sex?

And finally ... Ageing 'Ladyboys'

Kathoey are consumed by the maintenance of a 'beautiful' and youthful, 'feminine' appearance. Several *kathoey* prostitutes in their late twenties told me they worried that by the time they were thirty, they would be 'old and ugly' and that no-one would want them. They were concerned that their careers as sex workers would come to an end. Hence, I am intrigued to discover, *what happens to elderly Ladyboys?* My lines of enquiry in this regard were thwarted: it seems that no researcher has ever found any tangible evidence as to what happens to *kathoey* once they are too old to work in the sex industry, or, indeed, as successful cabaret performers. Moreover, although Thais I asked told me that some older *kathoey* give up the *kathoey* career and *'klap bahn'* [Trans: 'go home'], this notion was purely speculative and no-one was able to provide any evidence, anecdotal or otherwise, to substantiate their remarks. Sure enough, older *kathoey* cabaret performers take on the 'comedy' parts of cabaret shows, or they may work as seamstresses, making costumes for the shows. In fact, I saw two older *kathoey*, who looked to be in their late thirties to mid-forties, so employed. One was sewing costumes in an indoor market in Bangkok, the other working as a sales assistant in a costume shop in Pattaya. I have never, however, seen 'elderly' *kathoey*. Hence my enquiries as to the ageing *kathoey* are to be consigned to the subject of some future research.

ENDNOTE

It should be acknowledged that the research for this book was carried out some ten years prior to publication. Therefore, transitional procedures and processes could well have developed or changed. My findings here are not intended to criticise in any way the NHS or the Thai surgical industry, but simply to highlight the reported experiences of the transsexual women and kathoey who participated in the research.

BIBLIOGRAPHY

American Psychiatric Association (1994) *Diagnostic and Statistical Manuel of Mental Disorders (DSM-IV)*, Washington DC: American Psychiatric Association

Aull-Davies, C. (1999) *Reflexive Ethnography: A Guide to Researching Selves and Others*, London and New York: Routledge

Becker (1991:226) in Aull-Davies (1999) *Reflexive Ethnography: A Guide to Researching Selves and Others*, London and New York: Routledge

Benjamin, H. (1966/1999) Copyright of the electronic edition by Symposium Publishing, Düsseldorf, 1999. [Originally published by The Julian Press Inc, Publishers, New York (1966)]

Benjamin, H. *The Transsexual Phenomenon*, International Journal of Transgender URL: http://www.symposion.com/ijt/

Berreman (1969) in Aull-Davies (1999), *Reflexive Ethnography: A Guide to Researching Selves and Others,* London and New York, Routledge

Billings and Urban (1982) 'The Socio-medical Construction of Transsexualism — an Interpretation and Critique' in Ekins and King (eds) (1996), *Blending Genders: Social Aspects of Cross-dressing and Sex-changing*, London: Routledge

Bishop, R. and Robinson, L.S. (1998), *Night Market — Sexual Cultures and the Thai Economic Miracle*, New York and London, Routledge

Blumer, H. (1969) *Symbolic Interactionism: perspective and method*, Berkeley: University of California Press/Englewood Cliffs, N.J.: Prentice-Hall

Bolin, A. (1988) *In Search of Eve: Transsexual Rites of Passage,* USA: Bergin & Garvey

Bolin, A. (1993) 'Transcending and Transgendering: Male-to-Female Transsexuals, Dichotomy and Diversity': in Herdt, G (ed), *Third Sex, Third Gender, Beyond Sexual Dimorphism in Culture and History*, New York: Zone Books

Bornstein, K. (1994) *Gender Outlaws: On men, women and the rest of us*, New York: Routledge

British Medical Journal Editorial (1998), *1948: A turbulent gestation for the NHS. Some things don't change*, BMJ No. 7124 Volume 316 3 January

Brummelhuis, Han ten, (1999) 'Transformations of Transgender: The Case of the Thai *Kathoey* in Jackson, P.A. & Sullivan, G., *Lady Boys, Tom Boys and Rent Boys, Mail and Female Homosexualities in Contemporary Thailand*, New York: Harrington Park Press

Butler, J. (1990) *Gender Trouble: Feminism and the Subversion of Identity*, New York & London: Routledge

Coffey, Amanda (1999) *The Ethnographic Self: Fieldwork and the Representation of Identity*, London, thousand Oaks, New Delhi: Sage Publications

Cornwall, A. (1994) 'Gendered identities and gender ambiguity among travestis in Salvador, Brazil' in Cornwall, A. and Lindisfarne, N. (eds), *Dislocating Masculinity: Comparative Ethnographies*, London: Routledge

Dean, T. (2000) *Beyond Sexuality*, Chicago: University of Chicago Press

de Beauvoir, S. (1949), *The Second Sex*, London, Cape

De Laine, Marlene (2000) *Fieldwork, Participation and Practice*, London: Sage Publications

Denzin, Norman, (1992) 'Whose Cornerville is it, anyway?' *Journal of Contemporary Ethnography*, April Vol. 21 Issue 1, p120

Denzin (1997) in Mauthner et al (2002), *Ethics in Qualitative Research*, London, Sage Publications

Deuteronomy 22:v.5, *The New Jerusalem Bible: Study Edition* (1985/1994), London, Darton, Longman and Todd Limited

Diamond, M. (1982) Brief communication — 'Sexual Identity, Monozygotic Twins Reared in Discordant Sex Roles and a BBC Follow-up', *Archives of Sexual Behavior*, Vol. 11, No. 2

Diamond, M. (2000) 'Sex and Gender: Same or Different?' in *Feminism and Psychology*, vol. 10(1): 46-54

Douglas, M. (1966) *Purity and Danger: an analysis of concepts of Pollution and Taboo,* London: Ark Paperbacks

Edwards, R., (1993) 'An Education in Interviewing – Placing the Researcher and the Research' in Renzetti, C.M. & Lee, R.M. (eds.), *Researching Sensitive Topics*, London: Sage Publications

Ekins and King (1996) (eds), *Blending Genders: Social Aspects of Cross-dressing and Sex-changing,* London: Routledge

Ekins, R. (1997) Male-femaling: A grounded theory approach to cross-dressing and sex-changing, London & New York: Routledge

Ekins, R. (2005) 'Science, Politics and Clinical Intervention: Harry Benjamin, Transsexualism and the Problem of Heteronormativity', *Sexualities*, volume 8, number 3, July, pp.306-328

Ellis et al in Hertz, R. (ed) (1997) *Reflexivity and Voice*, London: Sage, California: Thousand Oaks

Freidson, E. (1970), *Professional Dominance*, New York: Atherton Press

Freidson, E. (1972), *The Profession of Medicine*, USA: Dodd, Mead and Company Inc.

Garfinkel, H. (1967) *Studies in Ethnomethodology,* Englewood Cliffs, N.J.: Prentice Hall

Goffman, Erving, (1959) *The Presentation of Self in Everyday Life,* USA: Anchor Books

Goffman, Erving, (1963) *Stigma – Notes on the Management of Spoiled Identity*, Englewood cliffs, N.J.: Prentice-Hall

Goffman, E. (1968) *Asylums: essays on the social situation of mental patients and other inmates*, New York, USA: Pelican Books

Halberstam, J. (2005) *In a queer time and place : transgender bodies, subcultural lives*, New York: New York University Press

Hausman, B.L. (1992) 'Demanding Subjectivity: Transsexualism, Medicine and the Technologies of Gender' in *Journal of the History of Sexuality*, Vol 3, No. 2

Herdt, G. (ed) (1993) *Third Sex, Third Gender: Beyond Sexual Dimorphism in Culture and History*, New York: Zone Books

Herdt, G. (1994) *Guardian of the Flutes, Vol. I: Idioms of Masculinity*, Chicago and London: University of Chicago Press

Hertz, R. (ed) (1997) *Reflexivity and Voice*, Thousand Oaks, California: Sage Publications

Hochschild, A.R. (1983) *The Managed Heart: Commercialization of Human Feeling*, London: Judy Piatkus

Home Office (2000) *Report on the Interdepartmental Working Group on Transsexual People.* London: Home Office. URL:

http@:www.lcd.gov.uk/constitution/transsex/, cited in Monro, S. and Warren, L. (2004) 'Transgendering Citizenship, *Sexualities* Vol. 7 No: 3 August, pp.345-362

Homer (1991) in Aull-Davies C. (1999) *Reflexive Ethnography: A Guide to Researching Selves and Others*, London and New York: Routledge

Jackson, P.A. (1995) *Dear Uncle Go: Male Homosexuality in Thailand*, Bangkok: Bua Luang Books

Jackson, P. A. (1997) 'Kathoey><Gay><Man: The Historical Emergence of Gay Male Identity in Thailand', in L.Manderson and M.Jolly (eds), *Sites of Desire-Economics of Pleasure: Sexualities in Asia and the Pacific*, Chicago, USA: The University of Chicago Press

Jackson, P.A. & Sullivan, G. (eds), (1999) *Lady Boys, Tom Boys, Rent Boys: Male and Female Homosexualities in Contemporary Thailand*, NY, USA: Harrington Park Press

Johnson, M. (1997) *Beauty and Power: Transgendering and Cultural Transformation in the Southern Philippines*, Oxford: Berg

Kenna, M.E. (1992) 'Changing places and altered perspectives: research on a Greek island in the 1960s and in the 1980s' in Okely J. and Callaway, H. (eds) *Anthropology and Autobiography*, London and New York: Routledge

Kessler, S.J. and McKenna, W. (1978) *Gender: An Ethnomethodological Approach*. New York, NY. John Wiley. Reprint 1985. Chicago, USA: The University of Chicago Press.

King, D., (1993) *The Transvestite and the Transsexual*, Aldershot, Hants: Averbury

King, D. (1996) 'Gender Blending — Medical Perspectives and Technology' in Ekins and King (eds), *Blending Genders: Social Aspects of Cross-dressing and Sex-changing,* London: Routledge

King, D. (2003) 'Gender Migration: a Sociological Analysis (or The Leaving of Liverpool)', *Sexualities*, vol. 6, No. 2, May 2003, pp.173-194

Klein (1998) 'From One 'Battle' to Another: The Making of a Travesti Political Movement in a Brazilian City', *Sexualities*, Vol 1(3):327-342, Sage publications

Kuiper, M and Cohen-Kettenis, P. (1988) 'Sex reassignment surgery: A study of 141 Dutch transsexuals', *Archives of Sexual Behavior*, 17(5):439-457

Kulick, D. (1996) 'Causing a commotion: Public scandal as resistance among Brazilian transgendered prostitutes' in *Anthropology Today*, Vol 12, No. 6

Kulick, D. (1998) 'Fe/male Trouble: The Unsettling Place of Lesbians in the Self-images of Brazilian Travesti Prostitutes', *Sexualities*, Vol 1(3):299-312

Kulick, D. (1998) *Travesti : sex, gender, and culture among Brazilian transgendered prostitutes*, Chicago: University of Chicago Press

Lang, S. (1998) *Men as Women, Women as Men*, Austin, USA: University of Texas Press

Lee, R.M. (1993/1999) *Doing Research on Sensitive Topics*, London: Sage

Lombardi, E.L., Wilchins, R.A., Priesing, D. & Malouf, D. (2001) 'Gender Violence: Transgender Experiences with violence and Discrimination', *Journal of Homosexuality*, Vol. 42(1)

Matzner, A. (2001) 'The complexities of 'acceptance': Thai students' attitudes towards kathoey', *Crossroads: An interdisciplinary journal of South East Asian studies, 15, 2, 71-93*

Mauthner, M., Birch, M., Jessop, J., & Miller, T. (eds) 2002) *Ethics in Qualitative Research*, London: Sage Publications

McCamish, M. (1999), 'The Friends Thou Hast: support Systems for Male Commercial Sex Workers in Pattaya, Thailand', in Jackson and Sullivan (eds), *Lady Boys, Tom Boys, Rent Boys, Male and Female Homosexualities in Contemporary Thailand*, New York, Harrington Park Press

McCloskey, Deirdre N. (1999) *Crossing — A Memoir*, Chicago & London: University of Chicago Press

Meyerowitz, J. (2002) *How Sex Changed: a History of Transsexuality in the United States*, Cambridge Massachusetts; London, England: Harvard University Press

Miller, J. (1982) 'People, Berdaches, and Left-handed Bears: Human Variation in Native America', *Journal of Anthropological Research*, Vol. 38, pp.274-87

Mitchell, J. (1974) *Psychoanalysis and Feminism — a Radical Reassessment of Freudian Psychoanalysis*, London: Penguin Books

Money, J. (1955) 'Hermaphroditism, gender and precocity in hyperadrenocorticism; psychological findings', *Bulletin Johns Hopkins Hospital* 96: 253-64, cited in Di Ceglie, D. (1995), 'Gender Identity Disorder in Children and Adults', *British Journal of Hospital Medicine*, Vol. 53, no. 6

Montgomery, H. (2001) *Modern Babylon? Prostituting Children in Thailand*, Fertility, Reproduction and Sexuality, Vol. 2, New York, Oxford: Berghahn Books

Montgomery, H.K. (2001b) 'Imposing Rights? A case study of child prostitution in Thailand' in Cowan, J.K., Dembour, M-B. and Wilson, R.A., *Culture and Rights — Anthropological Perspectives*, Cambridge: Cambridge University Press

Morgan, D. (1996) 'A Hitchhiker's Guide to Transsexualism', *Radical Deviance: A Journal of Transgendered Politics, March issue pp 4-5,* cited in Monro, S. and Warren, L. (2004) 'Transgendering Citizenship', *Sexualities* Vol. 7 No: 3 August 2004, pp.345-362

Moore, F. (2005), 'One of the Gals who's one of the Guys: Men, Masculinity and Drag Performance in North America' in Shaw and Ardener (eds), *Changing Sex and Bending Gender*, USA: Berghahn Books

Morris, J., (1997) [1974] *Conundrum*, London: Faber and Faber

Morris, R.C. (1994) 'Three Sexes and Four Sexualities: Redressing the discourses on Gender and Sexuality in Contemporary Thailand', *Positions* 2(1), 15-43

Nanda, S. (1993) 'Hijras: an Alternative Sex and gender role in India', in Herdt, G. (ed), *Third Sex, Third Gender, Beyond Sexual Dimorphism in Culture and History*, New York: Zone Books

Nanda, S. (1999) 'The Hijras of India: Cultural and Individual Dimensions of an institutionalised third Gender role' in Parker, R. & Aggleton, P. (eds) (1999), *Culture, Society and Sexuality*, A Reader, London: UCL Press

Nardi, P.M. & Schneider, B.E. (1998) *Social Perspectives in Lesbian and Gay Studies: A Reader*, London and New York: Routledge

Nettleton, S. (1995), *the Sociology of Health and Illness*, Cambridge, Polity Press

Oakley, A. (1981) 'Interviewing Women: A Contradiction in Terms' in H. Roberts (ed), (1981), *Doing Feminist Research*, New York: Routledge

O'Connell Davidson, Julia & Layder, Derek (1994) *Methods, Sex and Madness*, London & New York: Routledge

O'Connell Davidson, Julia (1998) *Prostitution, Power and Freedom*, Cambridge: Polity Press

O'Keefe, Tracie (1999) *Sex, Gender and Sexuality: Twenty-first Century Transformations*, London: Extraordinary People Press

Payer, L. (1996) *Medicine and Culture*, New York: Henry Holt and Company, Inc.

Plummer, K. (1975) *Sexual Stigma: An Interactionist Account*, London & Boston: Routledge & Kegan Paul

Plummer, K. (1995) *Telling Sexual Stories – Power, Change and Social Worlds*, London & New York: Routledge

Plummer, K. (2001) *Documents of Life-2: An Invitation to Critical Humanism*, London: Sage

Raymond, J. (1979) *The Transsexual Empire,* London: The Women's Press

Richards, R. (1983) *Second Serve: Renee Richards Story*, USA: Stein and Day

Rivett, G. (1998), *From Cradle to Grave. 50 Years of the NHS*, London: King's Fund Publishing

Roscoe, W. (1993) 'How to Become a Berdache: Toward a Unified Analysis of Gender Diversity' in Herdt, G., (ed), *Third Sex, Third Gender, Beyond Sexual Dimorphism in Culture and History*, New York: Zone Books

Said, E.W. (1978) *Orientalism*, London: Routledge & Kegan Paul

Scheper-Hughes, N. (1992), *Death Without Weeping: The Violence of Everyday Life in Brazil*, California: University of California Press

Shaffir, W.B., & Stebbins, R.A. (eds.) (1991) *Experiencing Fieldwork, An inside View of Qualitative Research*, London: Sage Publications

Sinnott, M. (1999) '*Masculinity and Tom Identity in Thailand*' in Jackson & Sullivan, *Ladyboys, tomboys and rent boys: Male and Female Homosexualities in Contemporary Thailand*. New York, USA: Harrington Park Press

Sinnott, M. (2004) *Toms and Dees: transgender identity and female same-sex relationships in Thailand*, USA: University of Hawai'i Press

Smyth, D. (1995) *Teach Yourself Thai: A complete course for beginners*, London: Hodder & Stoughton Ltd

Steiner Kvale (1996) in Mauthner M., Birch, M., Jessop, J., & Miller, T. (eds) 2002) *Ethics in Qualitative Research*, London: Sage Publications

Stoller, R. (1968) 'Male childhood transsexualism', *Journal of the American Academy of Child and Adolescent Psychiatry*, 7, 193-201.

Stoller, R. (1985) *Presentations of Gender*, New Haven and London: Yale University Press

Stoller, R. (1992) 'Gender identity development and prognosis: a summary', in C Chiland & J G Young (eds), *New Approaches to Mental Health from Birth to Adolescence* pp.78-87. New Haven, CT: Yale University Press

Stone, S. (1991) 'The Empire Strikes Back: A Posttranssexual Manifesto' in Epstein, J. & Straub, K. (1991) (eds), *Body Guards: The Cultural Politics of Gender Ambiguity*, London: Routledge, pp.280-305

Storer, G. (1999), 'Rehearsing Gender and Sexuality in Modern Thailand: Masculinity and male-male sex behaviours' in Jackson and Sullivan (eds), *Ladyboys, Tom Boys, Rent Boys, Male and Female Homosexualities in Contemporary Thailand*, NY, USA: Harrington Park Press

Suthrell, C.A. (2004) *Unzipping Gender: sex, cross-dressing and culture,* Oxford: Berg

Thayer, James S. (1980) 'The Berdache of the Northern Plains: A Socioreligious Perspective', *Journal of Anthropological Research* vol. 36, pp.287-293

Totman, R. (2003) *The Third Sex — Kathoey: Thailand's Ladyboys,* London: Souvenir Press

Trexler, Richard C. (1995) *Sex and Conquest: gendered Violence, Political Order, and the European Conquest of the Americas,* New York: Cornell University Press

Turner, V. (1967) *The Forest of Symbols: Aspects of Ndembu ritual* USA: Cornell University Press

Turner, Victor (1967) *'Betwixt and Between: The Liminal Period in Rites de Passage* in Victor Turner (ed), *The Forest of Symbols: Aspects of Ndembu ritual,* Ithaca, New York: Cornell University press.

Van Esterik, P. (2000) *Materializing Thailand,* Oxford: Berg

Van Gennep, A. (1908/1960) *Rites of Passage* translated by M.B. Vizedom and G.L. Caffee, London: Routledge and Kegan Paul.

Webster, C. (1998/2002 2nd Edition), *The Health Service — A Political History,* Oxford: Oxford University Press

West, C. and Zimmerman, D.H. (1987) 'Doing Gender' in *Gender and Society,* vol.1, No. 2, June, pp.125-151

Whitehead, Harriet (1981) 'The bow and the burden strap; a new look at institutionalized homosexuality in native North America', in Sherry B. Ortner & Harriet Whitehead (eds) *Sexual Meanings: The Cultural Construction of Gender and Sexuality,* Cambridge: Cambridge University Press

Whittle, S. (2002) *Respect and Equality: transsexual and transgender rights,* London: Cavendish Publishing Limited

Williams, Walter L. (1986) *The Spirit and the Flesh — Sexual Diversity in American Indian Culture,* Boston: Beacon Press

Willis, P. (2000) *The Ethnographic Imagination*, Oxford: Polity press in association with Cambridge and USA: Blackwell Publishing Ltd,

Zhou, J.N., Hofman, M.A., Gooren, L.J., & Swaab, D.F. (1995) 'A Sex difference in the human brain and its relation to transsexuality', *Nature*, 378, 68-70

Websites

Allyn, E (2002) *Buddhism in Thailand*, Floating Lotus Communications Co Ltd, and URL: www.Floatinglotus.com

Allyn, E. (undated) *How to Tell if a Barboy is Straight or Gay*, in http://www.floatinglotus.com/tmot/barboys.html accessed 28 February 2005.

(Anonymous) (2005) *C of E bishop gives backing to transsexual priest*, URL: www.ekklesia.co.uk 26 September

BBC-news (1998), *Stuffing their mouths with gold*, URL: http://news.bbc.co.uk/2/hi.events/nhs at 50/special report/119803.stm last accessed August 2006

Beaumont Society, URL: http://www.beaumontsociety.org.uk

Beaumont Society, Women of the, URL: http://beaumontsociety.org.uk/wobs

Benjamin, H. cited in Dr Harry Benjamin's Gender Disorientation Scale, URL: http://www,genderpsychology.org/transsexual/benjamin_gd.html Last accessed August 2004

British Medical Association (2006), *An Outline of the British Medical Association*, URL: http://www.bma.org.uk/ap.nsf/content/BMA outline History last accessed August 2006

Bunmi Methangkun. 1986 (2529). Khon Pen *kathoey* Dai Yaang-rai (How Can People be *kathoeys*?), Bangkok: Abhidhamma Foundation, cited in Jackson, P.A. (1996) *Non-normative Sex/Gender Categories in the Theravada Buddhist Scriptures*

URL:http://www.lib.latrobe.edu.au/AHR/archive/issue1-feb-mar-96/jackson/references.html sourced March 2005

Chanon Intramart and Allyn, E. (2003) *Ladyboys, Drag Queens and Gay Men on the Thai Silver Screen,* URL: http://www. floatinglotus.com/tmot/thaimovies6.html accessed 28 February 2005

Conway, Lynn, (2002) http://www.lynnconway.com/ last accessed August 2004)

DiCegli, D. (undated), URL: http://www.mermaids.freeuk.com/ dicegli.html, last accessed August 2006

European Court of Human Rights, *CASE OF X, Y AND Z v. THE UNITED KINGDOM,* Hudoc reference: REF00000619, Judgment (Merits), Application number: 00021830/93; Date: 22/04/1997 URL: http://hudoc.echr.coe.int/hudoc/

Floating Lotus URL http://www.floatinglotus.com/tmot/ thaimovies6.html

Gender Identity Research and Education Society (GIRES) URL: http://www.gires.org.uk/

GLBTQ — An Encyclopedia of Gay, Lesbian, Bisexual, Transgender and Queer Culture, URL: www.glbtq.com/social-sciences/ thailand.html

Gooren, (1993) URL: http//www.mermaids.freeuk.com/gooren01. html

Harry Benjamin Standards of Care URL: http:// www,genderpsychology.org/transsexual/benjamin_gd.html accessed June 2004

Home Office (2000) *Report on the Interdepartmental Working Group on Transsexual People.* London: Home Office. URL: *http@:www.lcd.gov.uk/constitution/transsex/,* cited in Monro, S. and Warren, L. (2004) 'Transgendering Citizenship', *Sexualities* Vol. 7 No: 3 August, pp.345-362

International Journal of Transgender URL: http://www.symposion. com/ijt/, last accessed May 2004

Jackson, P.A. (1996) 'Non-normative Sex/Gender Categories in the Theravada Buddhist Scriptures' in *Australian Humanities Review* URL:http://www.lib.latrobe.edu.au/AHR/archive/issue1-feb-mar-96/jackson/references.html sourced March 2005

Jackson, P.A. (2003) Performative Genders, Perverse Desires: A Bio-History of Thailand's Same-Sex and Transgender Culture in *Intersections: Gender, History and Culture in the Asian Context*, Issue 9 August, URL: http://wwwsshe.murdoch.edu.au/intersections/issue9/jackson.html

The Looking Glass Society (1997), *Electrolysis in Transsexuals* (2nd edition), November 1997, online booklet. URL: www.looking-glass,greenend.org.uk/electro.htm last accessed August 2006

Matzner, A. URL: http://home.att.net/~leela2/inlegallimbo.htm/ accessed 5 May 2002

Matzner, A. (2004), Citation information: Entry Title: *Thailand*, General Editor: Claude J. Summers, Publication name: glbtq: an *Encyclopedia of Gay, Lesbian, Bisexual, Transgender, and queer culture*, updated 31 December 2004, Publisher: glbtq Inc.

URL: www.glbtq.com/social-sciences/thailand.html sourced January 2004.

Matzner, A. URL: http://home.att.net/~leela2/politics.htm, sourced January 2004.

Mermaids URL: http//www.mermaids.freeuk.com/gooren01.html accessed January 2002

Press for Change URL: www.pfc.org.uk

Rakkit (1997) *The Nation*[49], 19 March, Focus Section, page 1 cited in

Matzner, A. (1999), *In Legal Limbo: Transgendered Men and the Law*, URL: http://home.att.net/~leela2/inlegallimbo.htm/ accessed 5 May 2002

---

49 *The Nation* is one of only two English Language newspapers printed in Thailand. The other newspaper is *The Bangkok Post*

Sinnott, M. (2002),'Gay vs. Kathoey: Homosexual Identities in Thailand', International Institute for Asian Studies Newsletter 29, special issue on Asian Homosexualities, November 15. URL: http://www.iias.nl/iiasn/29/ IIASNL29_7_Sinnott.pdf

Stryker, S. (2004), *Benjamin, Dr. Harry,* URL: http://www.glbtq. com/social-sciences/benjamin_h.html

Winter, S. (2002a), Research and Discussion Paper: *'Why are there so many kathoey in Thailand?'* last accessed July, 2004: URL:http://web.hku.hk/~sjwinter/TransgenderASIA/

Winter, S. (2002b), *'A Country Report'*, last accessed, August, 2004: URL: http://web.hku.hk/~sjwinter/TransgenderASIA/

Newspaper articles

Batty, D., (2004), 'Mistaken Identity' in *The Guardian Weekend* magazine, 31 July; pp.12-17

Hardy, R. (2004), 'I Never Want to be a Woman Again', *The Daily Mail*, 21 February

Southam, H. (2001) 'Ban sex change ops, says church', *The Independent on Sunday*, 14 January

Storrar, K. (2003), 'Biker chick — Stewart gives up hell-raising for a new life as sexy S...',*Daily Mirror*, 8 December

Taylor, D. (2003), 'He-she Rider — Hells Angel has sex-swap op', *The Sun*, 8 December, 2003

Veena T. & Parinyaporn, P. (2003), 'The Good Fight', *The Nation* newspaper, Bangkok, 28 November, 2003, p.4

Other Citations

Apirat Petchsiri, Professor of Law, Chulalongkorn University, Bangkok

Beaumont-Vernon, A. (2000) *Betwixt and Between: a cross-cultural comparative analysis of transgenderism,* unpublished MA Dissertation in Medical Sociology, School of Economic and Social Studies, University of East Anglia, UK

Brighton and Hove Lesbian, Gay, Bisexual and Transgender Community Strategy, Count Me In survey findings, report dated June 2001

Chaplin, B.J. (2004), *Tattoo Narratives: A Generational Study of the Changing meanings of the Tattoo,* unpublished PhD thesis, Department of Sociology, University of Essex, UK

Diagnostic and Statistical Manuals DSMIIIR (1980) and DSMIV (1994)

Green, R. (1999), citing Bellinger v Bellinger, Court of Appeal para 32, 2001, TLR 2000 cited in GIRES (2004), *Atypical Gender Development — A Review* — published in Great Britain by Gender Identity Research and Education Society (GIRES), Melverley, The Warren, Ashstead, Surrey KT21 2SP

Home Office (2000) *Report on the Interdepartmental Working Group on Transsexual People.* London: Home Office. *http@:www. lcd.gov.uk/constitution/transsex/,* cited in Monro, S. and Warren, L. (2004) "Transgendering Citizenship", *Sexualities* Vol. 7 No: 3 August 2004, pp.345-362

Jackson, P. (2005*), 'Performative Genders, Perverse Desires:* A Bio-History of Thailand's Same-Sex and Transgender Cultures' Research Seminar, 16 November, University College London

Kruijver, F. (2004), *Sex in the Brain: gender differences in the human hypothalamus and adjacent areas — relationship to transsexualism, sexual orientation, sex hormone receptors and endocrine status,* Graduate School Neurosciences, Amsterdam, Institute for Brain Research, Netherlands

Montgomery, H.K. (1995) *Public vice and private virtue, child prostitution in Thailand,* PhD thesis, Cambridge University

Parke, Jessica (2001) *Transgender Issues in the Far East and Legal Issues,* Transgender2001 Conference Report, University of East Anglia, Norwich September 2001 : pp83-84

Prempreeda Pramoj na Ayuttaya, *Internal dynamism of "Kathoei's Sexualities" in Modern Thailand,* a paper presented at the Third International Convention of Asia Scholars (ICAS3), 19-22 August 2003, Singapore.

Winter, Sam, Pornthip Chalungsooth, Teh Yik Koon, Nongnuch Rojanalert, Kulthida Maneerat, Wong Ying Wuen, Beaumont-Vernon, Anne, Loretta Ho M.W. (2004 forthcoming), *What do people think about transgender? A six-nation study of beliefs and attitudes.* A paper for presentation at the APQ Bangkok 2005 conference, July 2005

World Health Organization (WHO), Geneva, 1992, The ICD-10 (International Classification of Diseases) Classification of Mental and Behavioural Disorders.